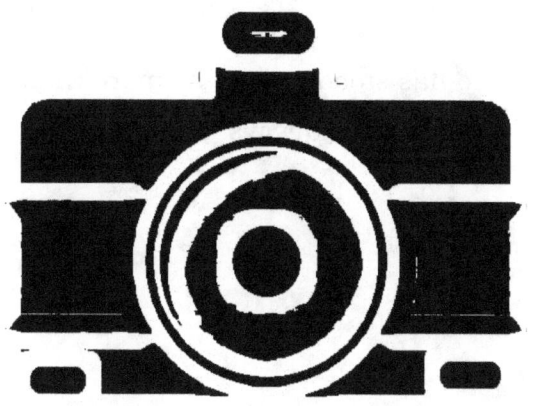

Reading

Writing

Listening

Speaking

Through the Lens of a

Camera

Martha Brady

To Travis who has stood quietly by more than all the rest.
And, as always, for Bubba

Table of Contents

Introduction

This book is a gigantic jumble of ideas, activities, and experiences that will work in almost any classroom, for any age child, with any ethnic background, in any economic status, and with any challenge that may present itself to the student, physically or mentally. It's about photos of every genre and age, some good, some exquisitely not so good. And it is about the ability of photos to engage children in ways other teaching tools simply cannot.

Photos can be magic to children. All the kids have to do is look and touch, and look again, and then make those pictures their own, any way they choose. And if THEY take the photos themselves, then the magic runs deeper. Notice the number of photos of my own animals in this book. That's how deep the magic is for me.

Having a digital camera in the classroom is like having another teacher, another aide, another social studies book, another math chart, another writing journal, and, quite simply, another tutor in the room. Photography is a personal event to the students; it gives them ownership, and it offers a way for the imagination to emerge, often before any Language Arts domain can come into play in an everyday scenario.

And remember, digital cameras can delete any unwanted photos, leaving only the best ones for students or pairs of students to use, enjoy, and become bewildered by. Crediting the photos they take or are taken by others is a lesson on ethics and responsibility as well.

The activities and experiences in the book are short, clean and to the point. For example, look at the photo after the Introduction. Put that photo on the overhead or smart board. The photo is of me taking my own shadow leaning into an oily puddle. Ask students what they THINK about the photo. Some may wish to write a poem of their own about the photo. Then, read the attached poem aloud. Let some volunteers give their interpretation and how those words connect to the photo itself. Are there metaphors or similes hiding somewhere? Is this poem an example of prose? Can this poem be rewritten to rhyme? Does it make sense to some students, and not to others? Why or why not? What word changes might occur to give it a better framework of understanding?

When doing these simple experiences with that simple poem, before you know it, a lesson is born that covers some standard, engages students in a meaningful way, and touches base with reading, writing, listening and speaking at the same time. Imagine, then, what will happen when you let students take their <u>own photos</u> for an assignment such as this one. The possibilities are, as they say, limitless.

In my past experiences as a classroom teacher I was so often guilty of giving diluted writing directions such as, 'Write about a cold, cold day', or, 'What did you do on your summer vacation', or worse yet, 'Write anything you care to write about". This kind of assignment often blocks the timid writer immediately. Some children have difficulty with 'creative vision' and therefore fail at writing before they even attempt to put words together. Photography, especially if it is personal, can be an authentic stimulus that brings success to such a student.

In this book you are going to see all kinds of photos. You will see photos so old they barely seem printable (sorry for that); some so trite you ask "why them?" There are photos of cat paws, aspen trees, airplanes, snow, fingers, sticks, and flowers. You'll see shots of old hands , people laughing, rabbits sitting on picnic benches, blankets in the woods, vacuum cleaners, floods, sleepy dogs, and many, many shots that seemed, at the moment, interesting. And that is the point...interesting. Children will, no matter what age, linger longer with you, stay in touch with your words, hold on to what's next, listen to all things possible, and maybe, just maybe, give you, and themselves, a gift of understanding, if they are interested.

Say Cheese could also be called the "Bubba" book because I used so many photos of my beloved Old English Sheepdog. Well, that's the way that is, and children will no doubt reuse their favorite photos of dogs or objects or friends over and over as well. It makes the heart warmer.

So, dear friends and educators, beg, borrow, or steal two or three digital cameras for your classroom. Get a printer that prints black and white photos on regular old paper in a decent manner (photo paper is cost prohibitive and color is an extra perk), and give your students time to touch, handle, examine, and use those cameras. Then, once they become familiar with the cameras, it is time to stand aside, SAY CHEESE, and bring renewed excitement, ownership, and authentic connection back into their own world of learning.

Enjoy!

MBrady

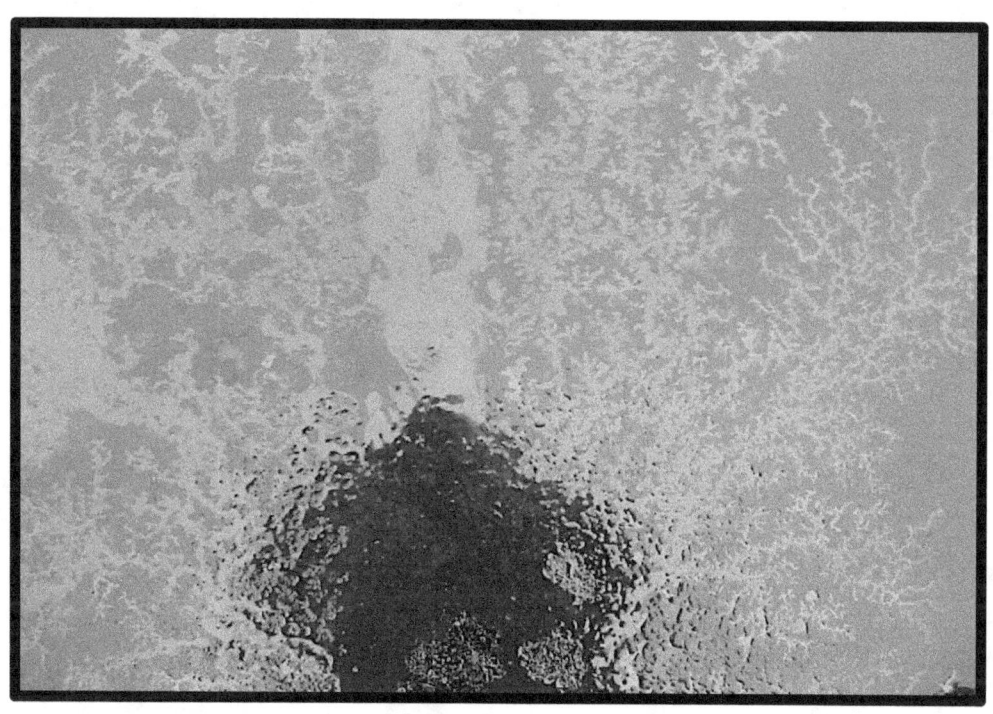

The sun spreads its form through the crevices
of the mind and the colors bleed and
blend into the imagination like oil
I swim the length of that captured moment
and pick up a pen
and write
Author

1
A Child Is

The moment a little boy is concerned with which is a jay
and which is a sparrow, he can no longer see the birds or hear them sing.
Eric Berne

☛*Students will add describing words to self-photos.*

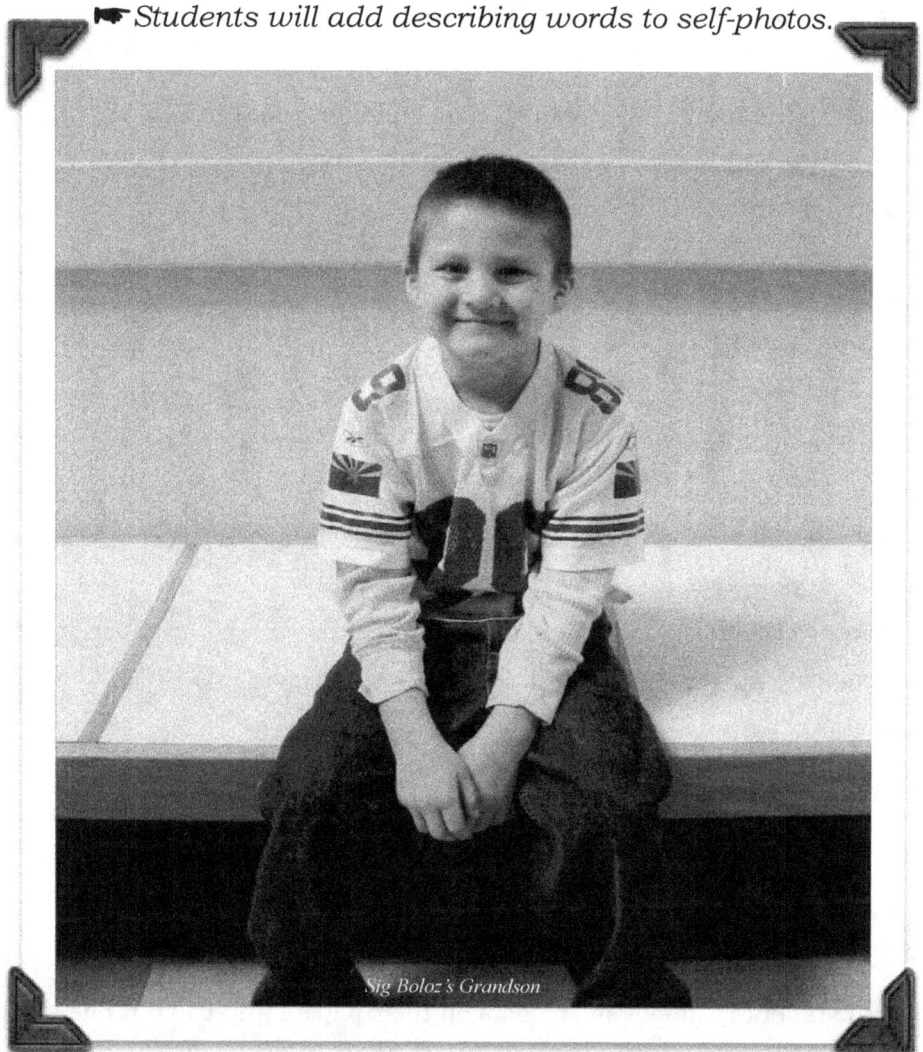

Sig Boloz's Grandson

A Child is....

run, arms, sky, chaos, wings, summer, rain, ball bat, frogs, talk, wonder, bicycle,
somersault, ice cream, steak, skipping, pizza, freckles, teeth, cartoons, gloves, comic
books, leaves, elbows, knees, dash, spin, kites, worms, dogs, trucks, football, worry,
space, grin, grimace, twirl, dirt, rumpled, instant glue,
A Child is ... a boy

Here We Go!

❑ Pick 5 things in the classroom (book, pencil sharpener, backpack, etc.) Students will describe them.

❑ Select an object or event that students will use to complete this sentence; The (shoes) are ___and___.

❑ Teacher stands in the front of the room as each child describes him or her in appropriate ways.

❑ Someone writes those descriptive words on the board as they are called out. appropriate ways.

❑ Discuss any words that are unknown.

❑ Depending on the grade level, these words will be divided into Nouns, Adjectives and Verbs.

❑ Each child will create a space, inside or out, where he or she wants to be photographed.

❑ In pairs, students will photograph each other in the desired locations (in desks, swings, etc.)

❑ Students will print their own 4x6 black and white photos on regular paper and staple on black construction paper. Students will staple a white sheet of paper at the bottom of the construction paper.

❑ Photos will be displayed in room and students, at random, will go to the displays and one appropriate word that best describes each of their classmates.

What Else Can We Do

✳Pick out 5 words and write a paragraph using those words.

✳Say VERB and students will look at the lists on their papers and call out one verb they see.

✳Students take photos of parents and do this activity as a Christmas or Birthday gift for them.

✳Take photos of inanimate objects and write sentences using descriptive words they have listed.

✳Students will journal this question, "The 3 words that I would like to add to my personal descriptive list are ___, ___, and ___ because_____."

✱With a self-portrait, label several parts on the photo that *define who you are.* Example:

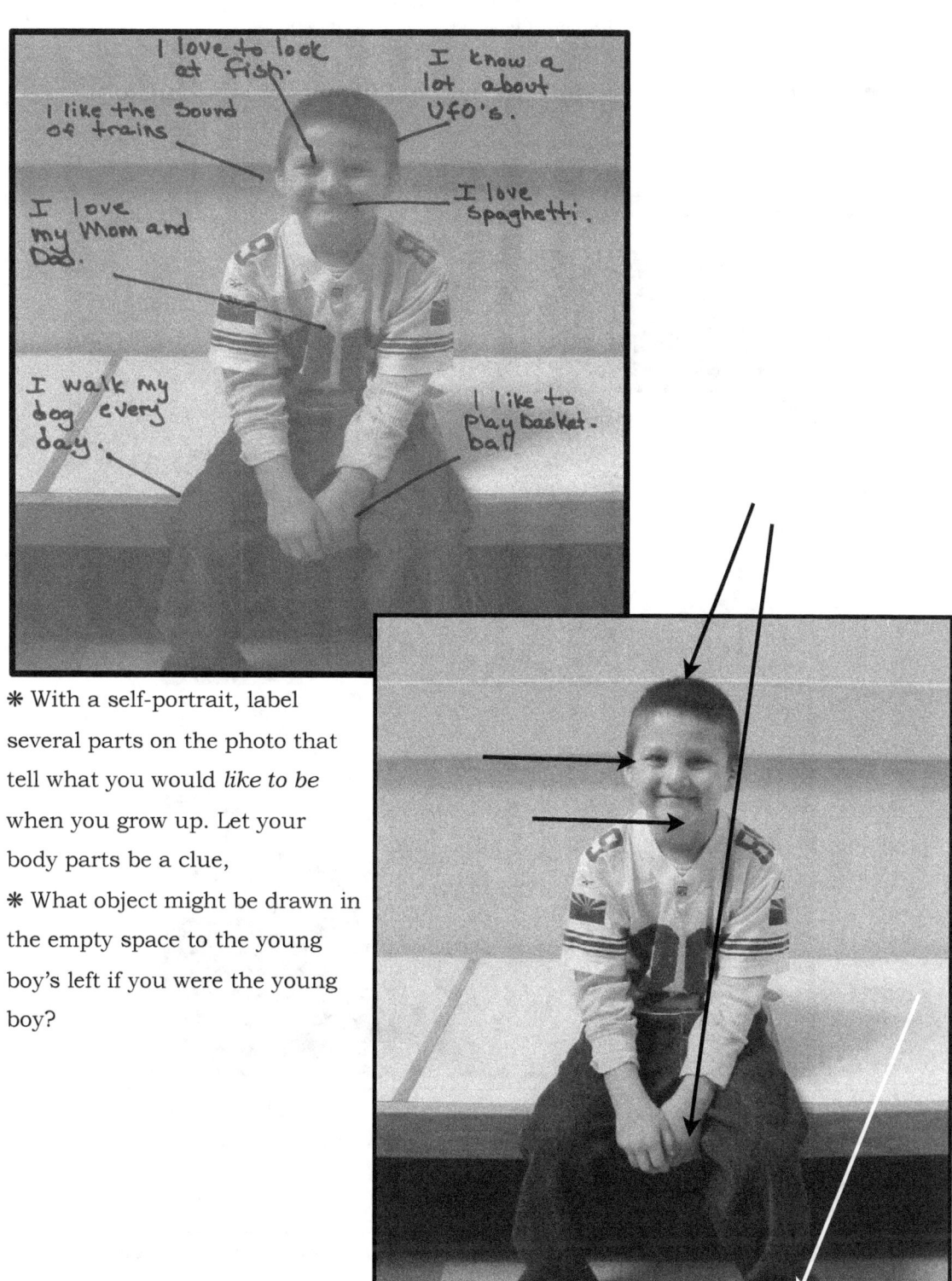

✱ With a self-portrait, label several parts on the photo that tell what you would *like to be* when you grow up. Let your body parts be a clue,

✱ What object might be drawn in the empty space to the young boy's left if you were the young boy?

2
Add-On-Stories
It takes a thousand voices to tell a single story.
Native American Saying

☛ *Students will write Add-On Stories using sequential photos.*

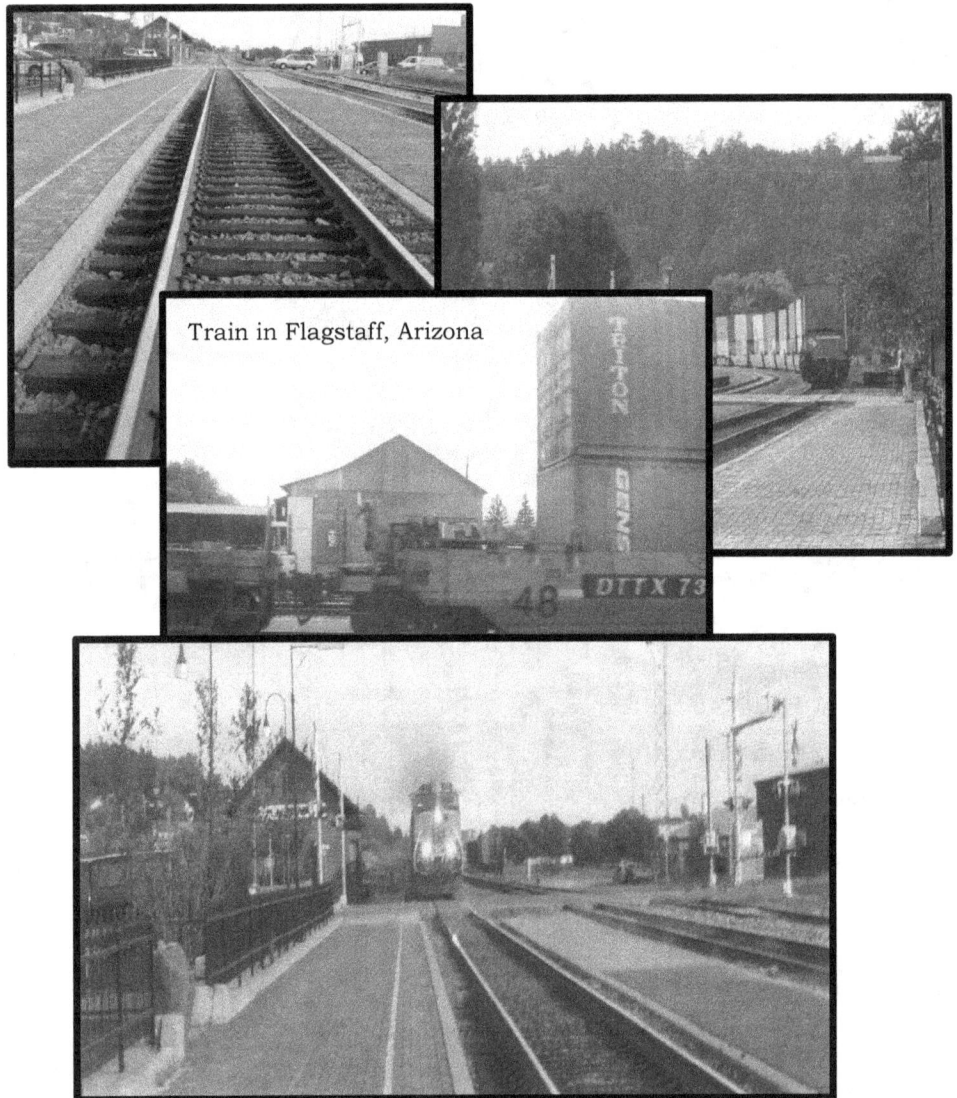

Train in Flagstaff, Arizona

Add – On stories are sequential stories written by several people. Each person has a particular part in the story. They may be written in a variety of styles while incorporating writing skills at all levels and ages.

Review the 6 elements needed for a good add-on story: beginning action, description

Here We Go

❏ Students will brainstorm various ideas that embellish the 6 elements. Put these on the board.

❏ Using the 6 elements, six students will *tell* an add-on story that focuses on the train photos on the previous page.

❏ Read the following beginning sentences. Students will brainstorm opinions of what the 6 elements would be in each scenario:

> ***From far, far away, I saw a brilliant light that seemed to be moving toward me.**
>
> ***On the 3rd day of our boat trip, I accidentally tripped and fell off the side of the boat, into the water.**
>
> ***One night, while I was walking down the hall to my room, I**

❏ Give students 15 minutes to get into voluntary groups and write a short add-on story from one of the scenarios.

❏ Now each group will take ONE photo that is conducive to add-on storytelling.

❏ Groups will swap photos, assign elements in their groups, and begin writing photo appropriate add-on stories. The assignment can be a sentence per element, or a short paragraph, depending on the age of the students involved. Eventually they will reflect on the personal ease or difficulty of the assignment.

❏ Groups will show their specific photos to the rest of the class and ask them to brainstorm what their add-on story may be about. Each group will then read their stories.

❏ Students will display all of the photos in a bulletin board setting and each student will select one photo and use that photo to write a mystery paragraph or a story without an end.

What Else Can We Do

✳ Using two copies of the bench photo, cut out pictures from the newspaper and tape one on each bench.

Pairs of students will write a short story that begins and ends on the bench.

✳ Research the history of 5 train stations somewhere in your state or the United States.

✳ Each student will draw one train car with windows. Students will place a self-portrait in the window of their own train car. Staple the train cars on a wall. As an ongoing project, students, singularly or in pairs or groups, will write add-on stories about the trip they are taking. The bench must be part of the story.

✳ Place these clues for good story writing on the board. (*Courtesy of Sig Boloz*)

> *Beginning: action, dialogue, questions, sound effects*
>
> *Setting: 5+1 w's, 5 senses*
>
> *Suspension: slow down action; get inside main character's head*
>
> *Main event: see beginnings*
>
> *Conclusion: find a way to end it*
>
> *Satisfying ending: memories, feelings, hopes, wishes, and growth*

✳ Student will share their writings, defining one particular element.

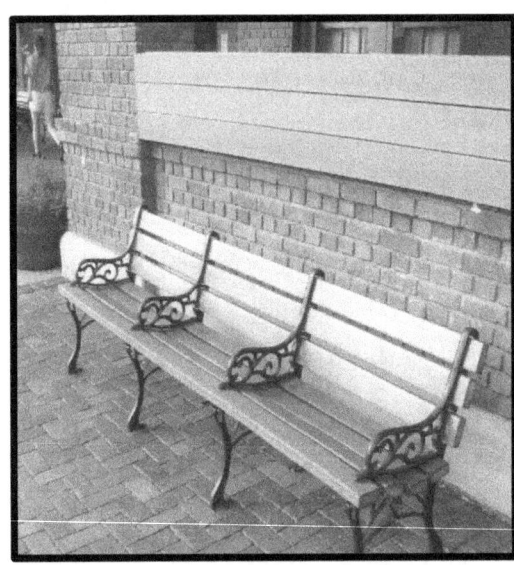

3
Alphabetizing

My alphabet starts with this letter called yuzz.
It's the letter I use to spell yuzz-a-ma-tuzz.
You'll be sort of surprised what there is to be found
Once you go beyond 'Z' and start
Poking around.
Dr. Seuss

☞ *Students will use photos as stimuli for writing descriptive*
words and nouns in a narrative format, focusing on 1ˢᵗ letter alphabetizing.

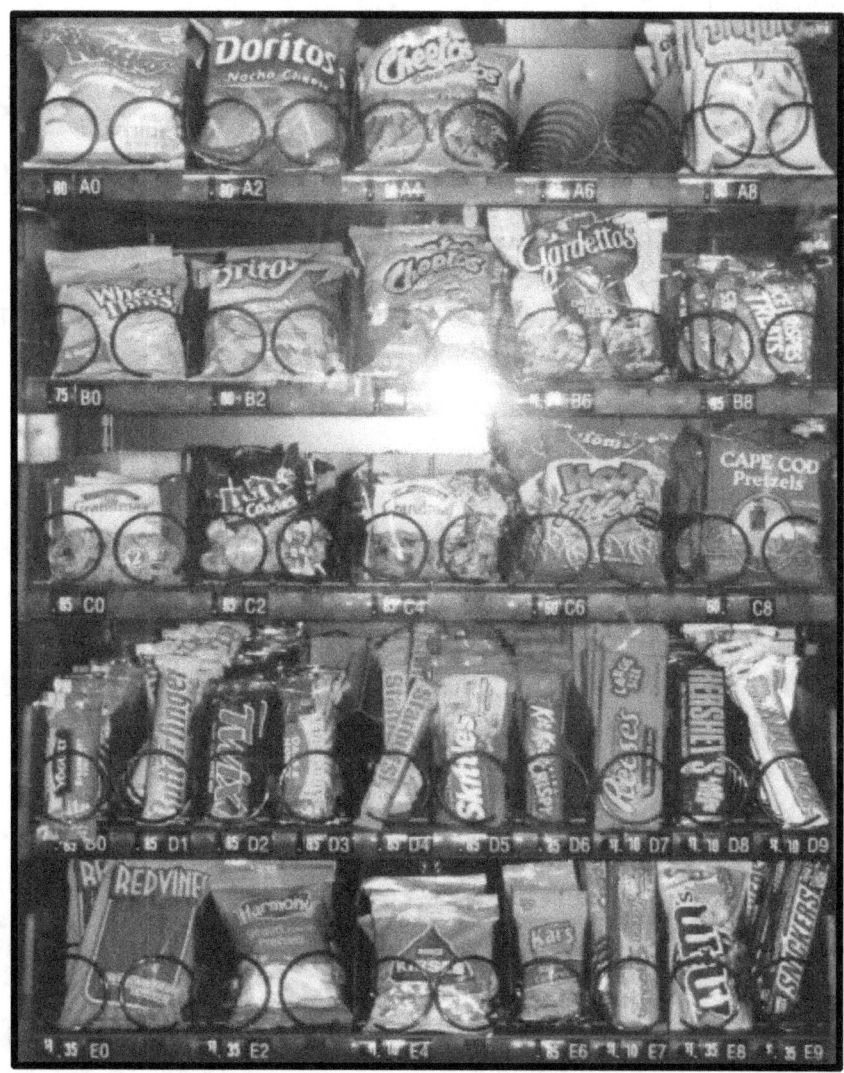

❑ Students will read a copy of this story and will look at the photo of the candy machine and find all the **bold** words that are seen in the photo or connect to other words seen in the photo. They will circle as many words as can been seen, right on the photo.

*I look into this wonderful **machine** that looks like a **television,** and there are **zillions** of pieces of candy and treats to choose from. Some have **raisons,** which add some kind of **nourishment**, and others have **peanuts**. There are even some that are **white**. There is **enough junk** in these **bags** to open up an antique store.*

*Just look at the **Hershey Kisses** glaring at us. I guess my favorite snack is found in **A-2.** I love **Doritos**. If they had a little bit of **icing** on them they would be even better. **Funyums** are good too, but if we **x-rayed** our insides we would probably see them wrapped around our intestines. That would **upset** my stomach so much that I might even stop eating this **stuff.** Perhaps the red **licorice** would solve the problem. **Wheat Thins** that come in a **solid yellow** sack may be a little healthier for us, but none are low in calories, even **Grandma's** treats that are on C-4.*

*I wonder if any of these snacks have **vitamins?** Oh, who cares? Give me some money **quick** so I can **open** up one of these little prizes now.*

❑ When the words are seen, students will write those words on the board and put them in ABC order.

❑ Students will shoot a generic photo.

❑ In pairs or individually, students will write a story about the generic photo.

❑ The story will include as many adjectives or nouns that begin with the first letter of the alphabet as possible.

❑ The alphabetical worlds will be underlined or highlighted in some way in the body of the story.

❑ Allow students to set their own goals of how many alphabetized words they can ❑ Students will read each other's stories and find the alphabetized words somewhere in the photo.

What Else Can

✳With a partner, go to the playground or in front of the schoolyard and take a *nature shot* similar to the one on the following page.

✳ Blow up the photo below on the overhead and see if the boys and girls can find V,Y,W,L, I, A and a tweaky little o. There are others for sure

✳Show them the hidden K to get them started on this fun alphabet adventure,

✳ Look for hidden letters of the alphabet in the photo and select one letter.

✱ Write a *nature* sentence, paragraph, story (fact or fiction), using that letter to begin the writing piece.

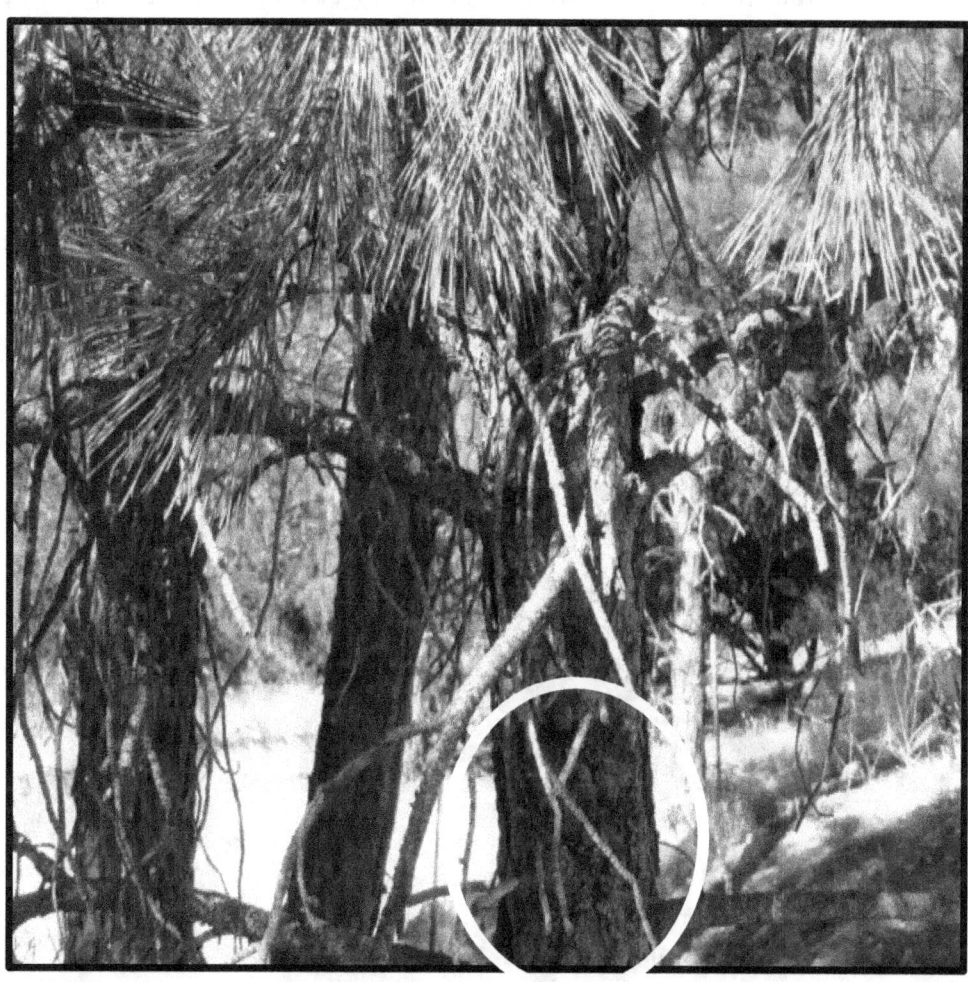

4
Angles
(Point-of-View)

"Prose is architecture, not interior decoration."
— Ernest Hemingway

☛ *Students will write a 3rd person **point-of-view** paragraph using a particular angle of a particular object in a photo.*

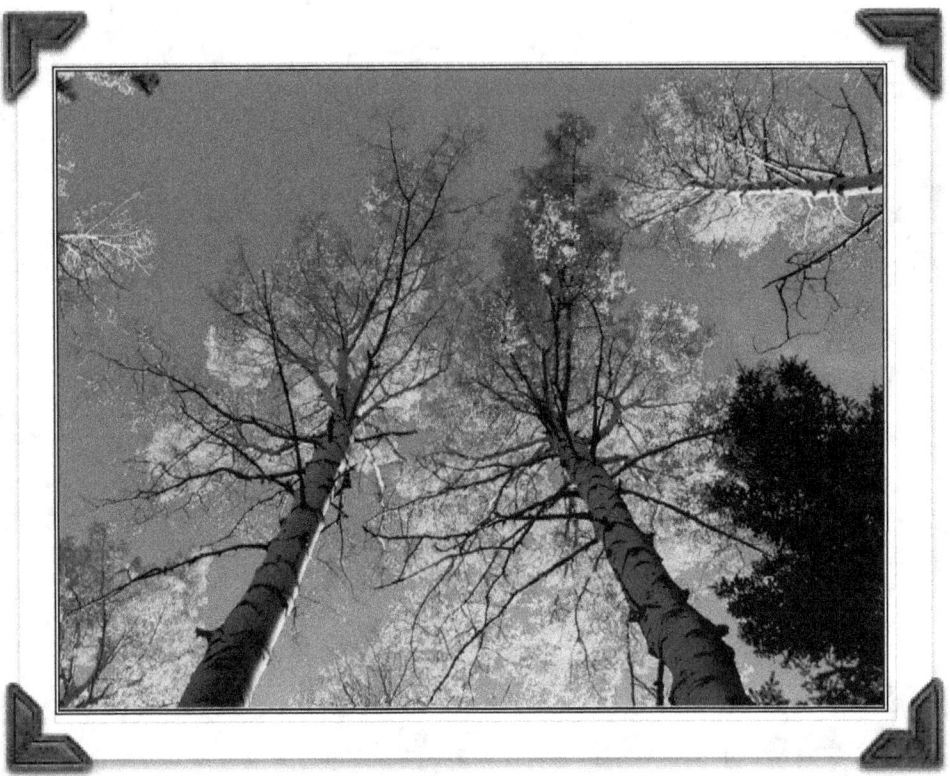

The sun rests on the leaves of Aspens

And waits for the wind to carry them,

Like doubloons from a thousand pirate ships,

To the velvet ground

Below

Author

Point-of-View is the **angle** and placement from which we view a photo. In <u>writing</u>, when we write a story we must decide from what <u>angle</u> or 'voice' the readers hear the story.

Here We Go!

❏ Show a photo of an object, such as the Aspen grove shot on the previous page. Discuss the photo's varied physical elements (sky, cloud, leaves, trunk 'eye', bark, limbs, shadows, etc,).

❏ Students will find ONE landscape, still life, or natural spot to 'shoot'.

❏ They will shoot different angles of that one object or landscape.

❏ Suggested writing ideas include:

What is not seen? What is the mood of the shot? How does a close-up shot create your writing idea? How does a far-off shot create your writing idea? What questions come to mind about your particle angle/voice? What and where is the mystery of the object? What does the background say? Is there a relationship between your 'voice' and some other part of the photo? How does a downward shot reveal more voice substance? How does

❏ Students will use their 3rd person writing pieces to brainstorm changing them into 1st or 2nd person 'voices' or point-of view/angle stories.

❏ Students will use their 3rd person writing pieces to brainstorm changing them into 1st or 2nd person 'voices' or point-of view/angle stories.

❏ Students will pick random objects in the classroom and practice 1st, 2nd, and 3rd 'voice' point-of-view sentences relating to their own lives.

❏ Students will read the poem about the Aspens on the previous page and discuss how parts of the tree come to life

What Else Can We Do

✳ Add *adjectives, movement, end results, inanimate pov, or comfort* to angle shots and point-of-view stories by showing photos that elicit some kind of emotion on which the writer can easily see and write.

✳ Add nouns, pronouns, verbs, adverbs, prepositional phrases, metaphors, similes, or any other parts of speech to create point-of-view writing experiences.

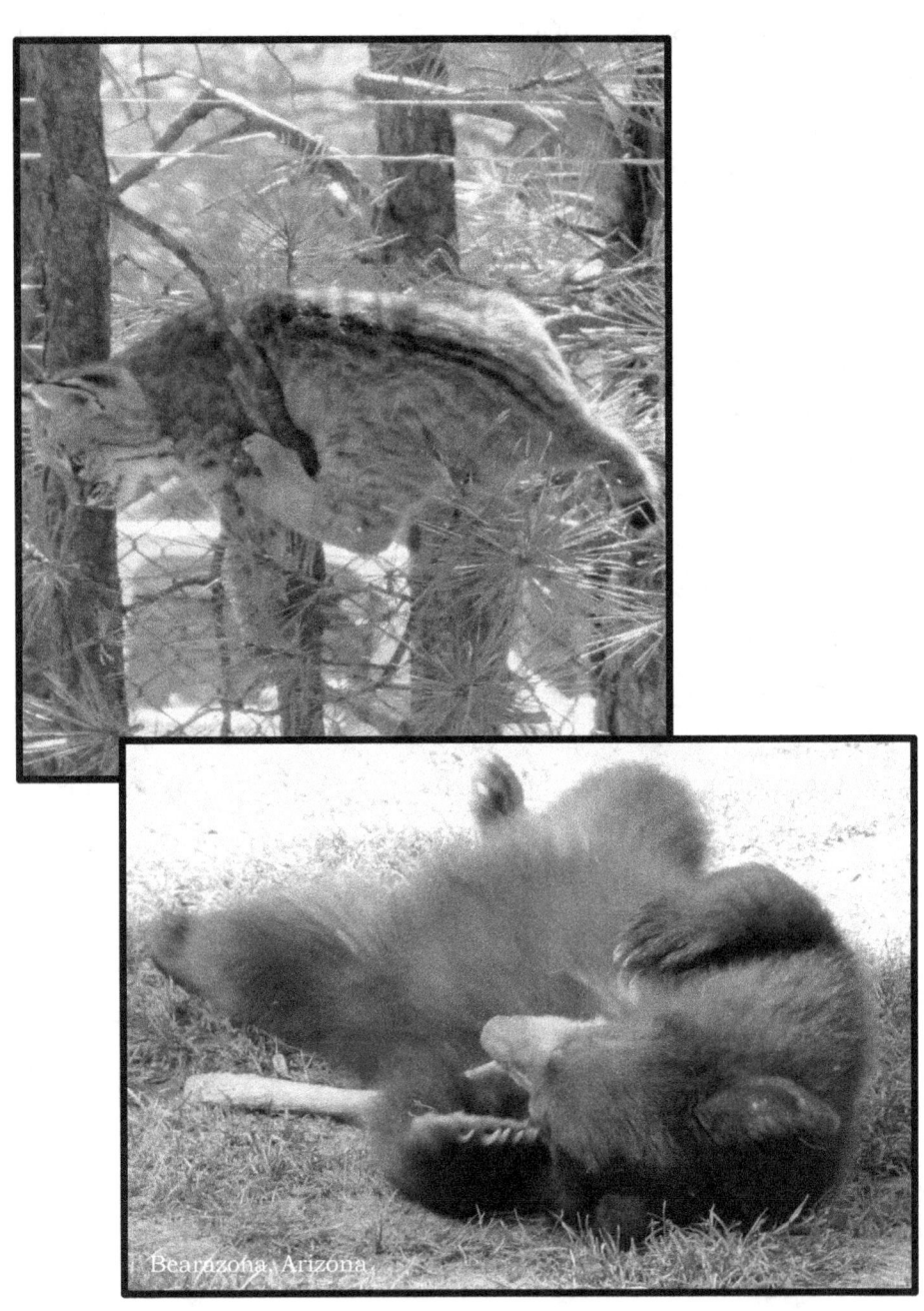

Bearizona, Arizona

5
Animal Captions
Never feed a cat anything that clashes with the carpet.
Jeroen Kessels

☞ *Students will write one-sentence captions to accompanying photos.*

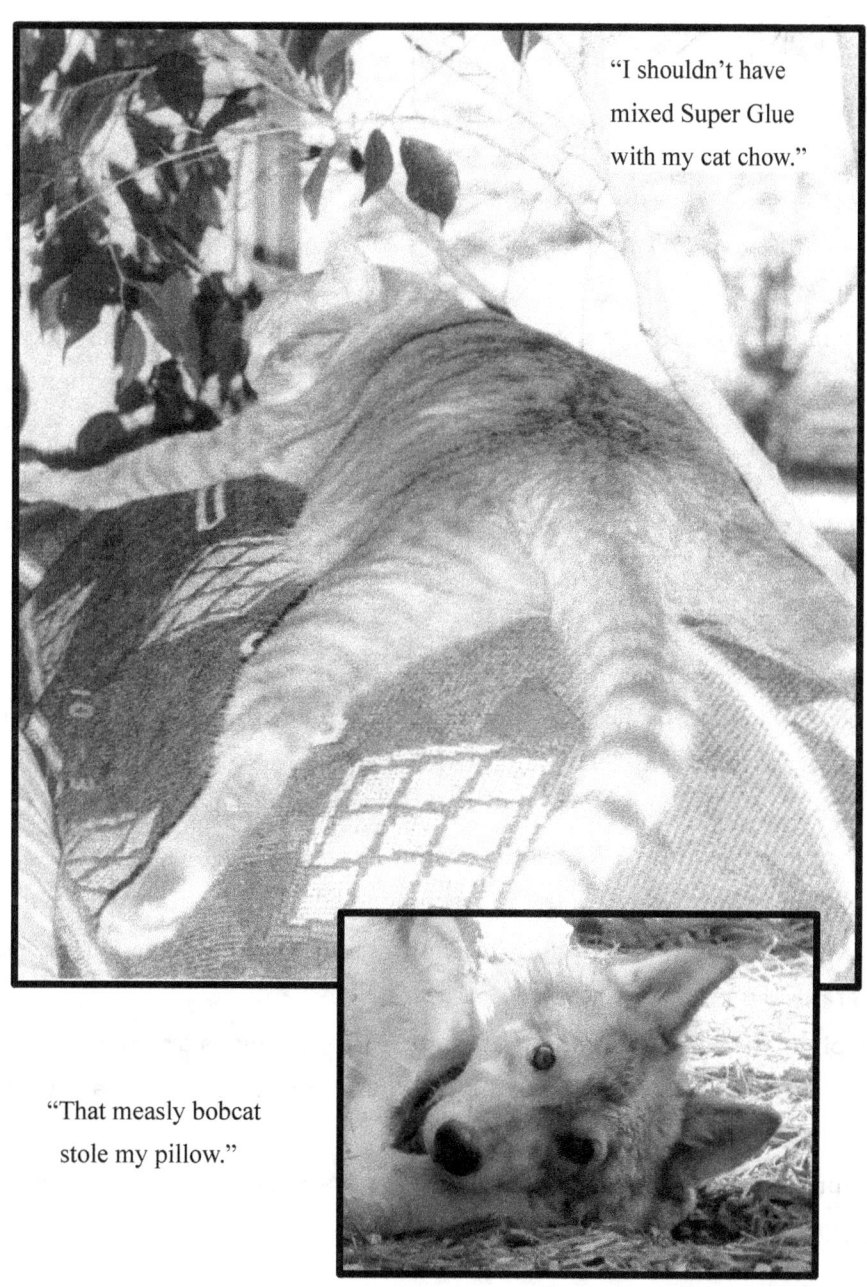

"I shouldn't have
mixed Super Glue
with my cat chow."

"That measly bobcat
stole my pillow."

Here We Go!

❏ Before hand, students will be asked to bring a stuffed animal to class, if possible.

❏ Use the photo on the previous page as catalysts for talking about or comparing personal pets.

❏ Define the word *caption* (A title, short explanation, or description accompanying an illustration or a photograph.)

❏ Ask students to look at the photos and create a: (1.) describing caption (2.) factual

❏ In groups of 3, students will create 1st, 2nd and 3rd person captions about one of the

❏ Look at captions under each photo. Students will determine the meanings as they apply to the photo itself.

❏ Students will pair up and photograph their stuffed animals in a setting they create.

❏ The same pair of students will write funny 1st person captions under their selected photos.

❏ Pairs will then discuss the process that led to the completion of their assignment.

❏ Students will display work in the hallway bulletin board designed for photography assignments.

What Else Can We Do

✱ Use the photos of the cat and the fox on the previous page to create two charts, one labeled WILD ANIMALS, and one labeled DOMESTICATED ANIMALS. Students will research one interesting fact about each of these animal types. These facts will be added to the chart and shared with the class.

✱ Create a personal or group KWILT chart (what I know, what I want to know, how I intend to learn, and how I will teach what I know to others) one of the two types of animals. Take a photo of that particular animal in real life, in a magazine or book or off of a TV program to use as your catalyst for this assignment.

✱ Choose a photo and caption from a newspaper. Bring to class and discuss how the *caption* of the photo enhances, explains, or improves or clarifies the meaning of the photo.

✱ Write a caption to the photos again as if they were seeing a: Hunter, Sheep, Wolf Cub, Bear, Man, Bicycle, Pizza, or Horse.

6
Arrays

The limits of my language are the limits of my mind. All I know is what I have words for.
Ludwig Wittgenstein

☛ *Students will review and use linear arrays and photos to expand vocabulary and create word relationships.*

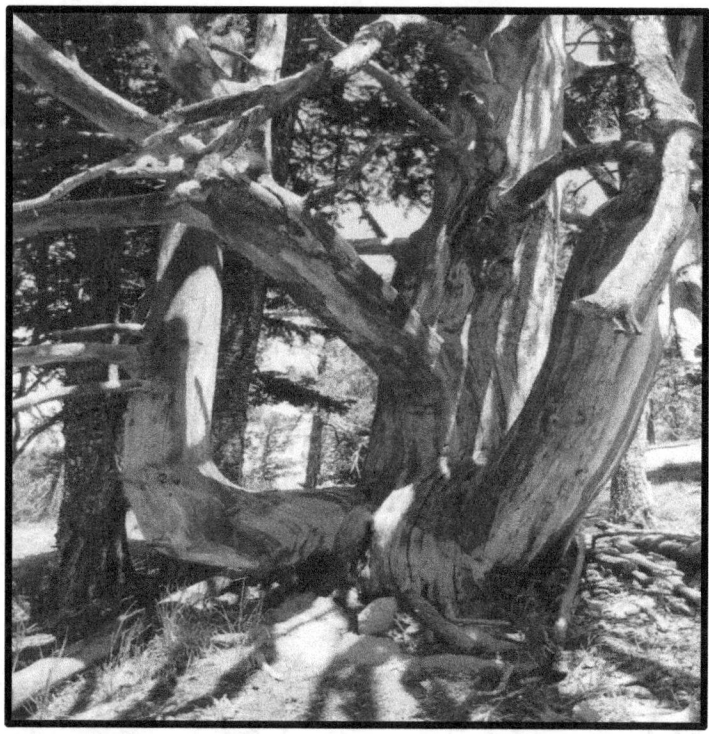

Using Linear arrays is a strategy to extend vocabulary by asking students to extend their understanding of words. Using opposites on each end, students add words to extend their understanding of words. Using opposites on each

Straight	Bent	Crooked	Gnarly	Knotted
Bright				Dark

Here We Go!

❏ Discuss the definition of *arrays* and also the definition of *degree* and *order* as they apply to word relationships.

❏ Show the following array as it applies to the tree on the previous page. Students will discuss the words in the array and if the *degree and order* are correct.

❏ Students will use an expanded vocabulary to create a story about the tree.

❏ One student will take a picture of something in the room (desk, sink, jacket, bulletin board, etc.)

❏ The class will create a 3-lined community linear array with 4 squares in each line.

❏ Each student will use newly connected words to write a paragraph about the object in the photo.

What Else Can We Do

✳ Look at this old tree and let students fill in this array that must include other words for "big". Student will then write a story using two animate and three inanimate characters in the story that can be described as one of the synonyms for 'big'.

✳ Now try to create an array with the word *old*.See how far you can go. This time, tell your story instead of writing it.

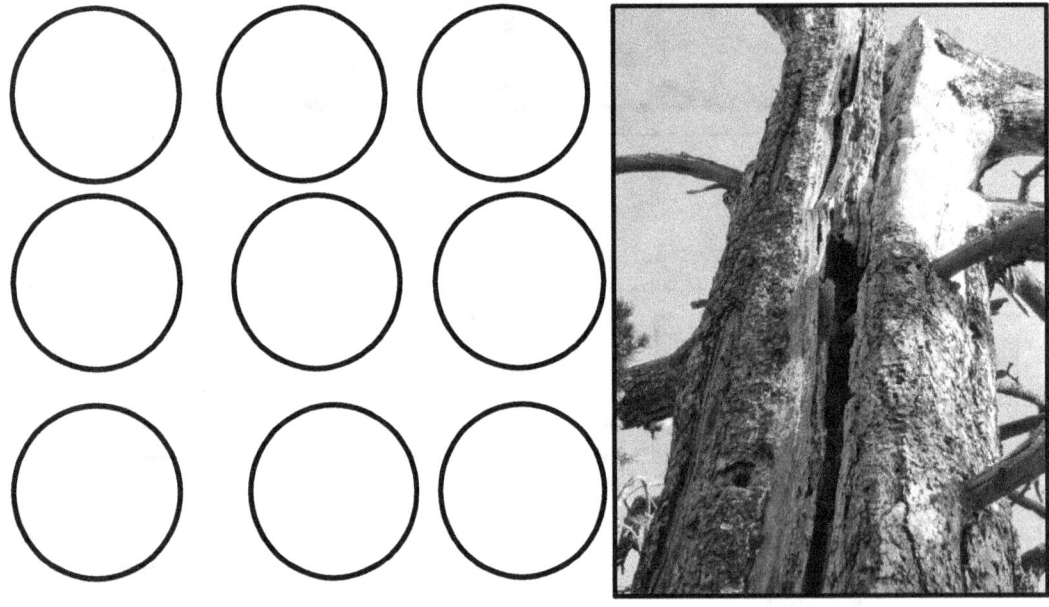

7
Belonging

The earth is what we all have in common.

Wendell Berry

☛ *Students will use "I think' questions to 'read' a nature photo to find things that connect.*

☛ *Students will use photos to talk about how, why and where things belong.*

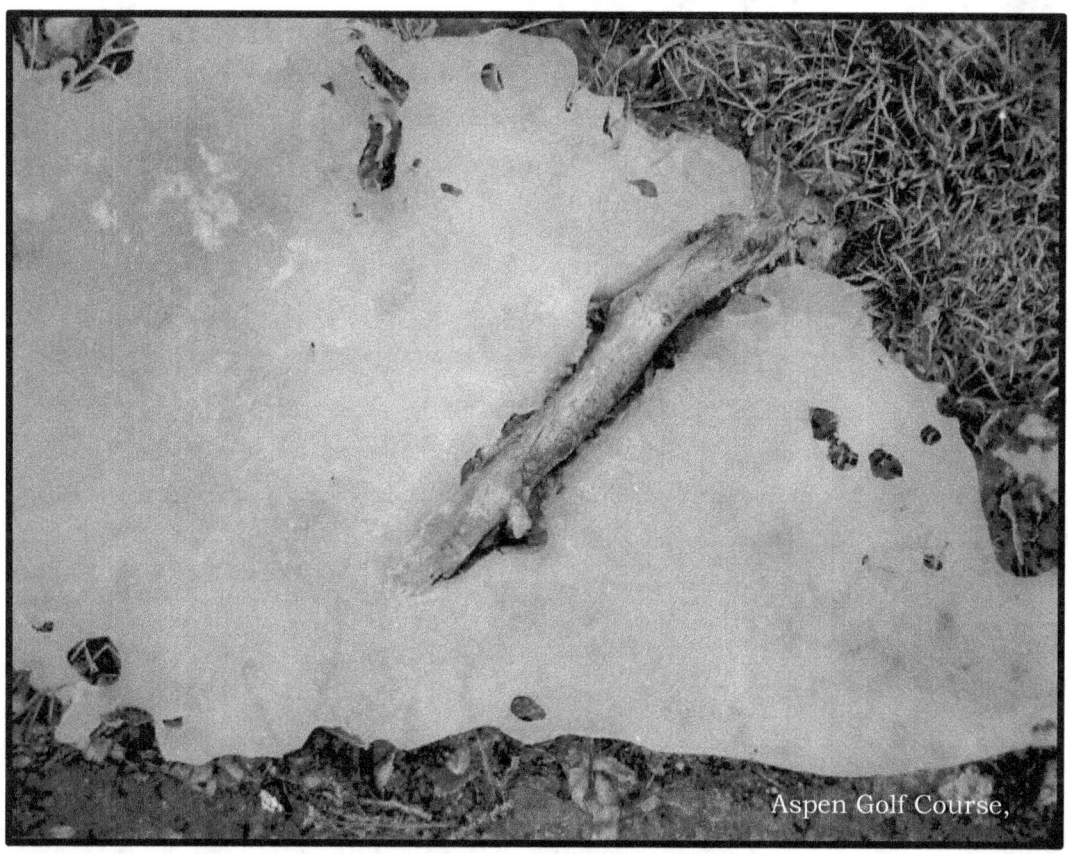

Aspen Golf Course,

Lead a class discussion about *belonging* Family, Classroom,
School, Neighborhood, City, State, Country, Earth, and the Universe.

Here We Go!

❏ Look at the photo and ask students how the photo came to be, what the two objects have in common, and why they belong together.

❏ Look at the photo and ask students how the photo came to be, what the two objects have in common, and why they belong together.

❏ Talk about one part of the photo that appeals to you.

❏ Use your 5 senses to 'read' the photograph. How do your 5 senses 'belong' to that photo?

❏ Teach a lesson on one aspect of the photo and how it 'belongs" to the planet.

❏ Ask students to begin a sentence *I think...* and relate the sentence to the photo.

❏ Create an abstract drawing and show how it *reflects* your feelings about the photo.

❏ Become the photographer of this particular photo. Where would YOU want the viewer to pay attention?

❏ Tell a story about this photo using different endings.

❏ Read this photo in mathematical terms.

What Else Can We Do

✻ Take a photo of you and your best friend, or you and your pet, or you and your family, or you and your____.   Simply talk about why you *belong* in that photo with that person, or dog, or family.

✻ Now take a walking tour of your school and have kids jot down things or people they see that *belong*.

✻ Come back to class and talk about the *bigger* and *smaller* picture of *belonging*.

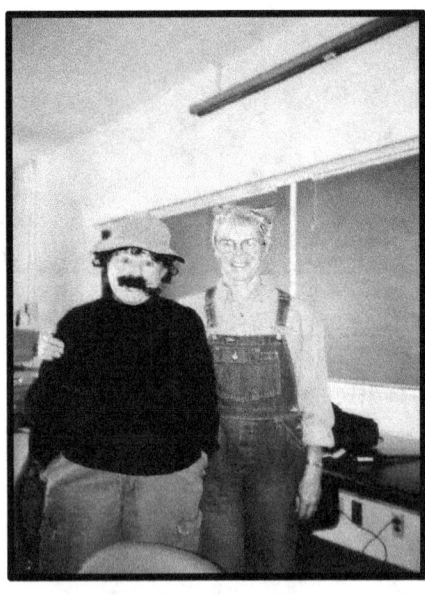

Old friends, "Geraldo Rivera" and "Rosie the Riveter"

8
Best of Show

Did you ever notice when you blow in a dog's face he gets mad at you?
But when you take him in a car he sticks his head out the window.
Steve Bluestone

☛ *Students will use one interesting animal photo as a stimulus for a writing piece.*

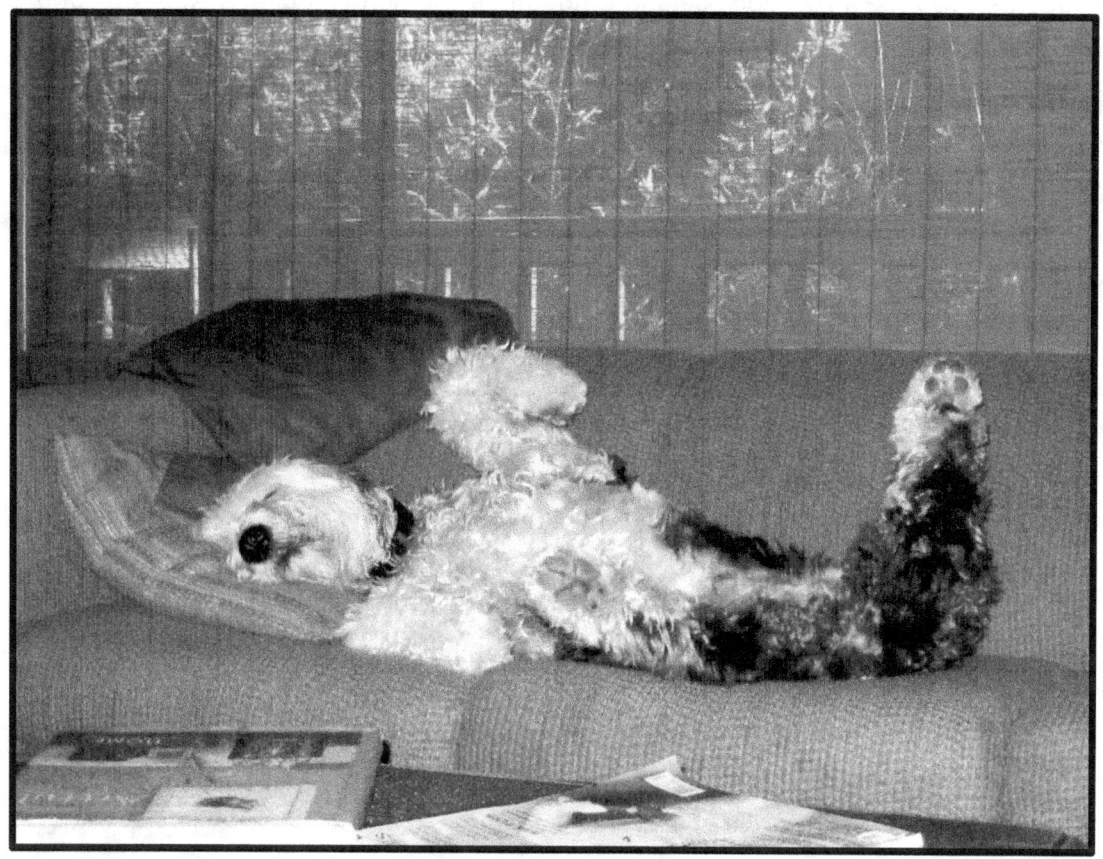

Bubba on Vacation in Oregon

Here We Go!

❑Students will take photos or bring to class photos of one or all of their animals. Over time they may choose one of the following projects, some of them, or all of them, depending on age appropriateness

❑Students will write a Didactic poem, a Cinquain, a Diamonte, a Limerick, or any of the other types of poems.

❑Students will write stories about their animals with an *open ending* so that others can complete it.

❑Students will write a *fictional story about* their animal(s).

❑ Students will research and write 10 facts about their animal(s).

❑4 students will create puppets of their animals and write and perform a combined puppet script.

❑Students will write a commercial that features their animal(s).

❑ On slips of paper in 3 baskets, the teacher will write 5 possibilities each, for these 3 story elements: *setting, time period,* and *situation.* Students will pick one slip from each basket and write a story incorporating those three elements in a story. The *character,* of course, *will* be one of their animals.

What Else Can We Do

✻ After a lesson on myths, students will write a Native myth, a Japanese myth, a Creation myth or an Aesop's Fable, about this insect or an insect or spider of which students take photos.

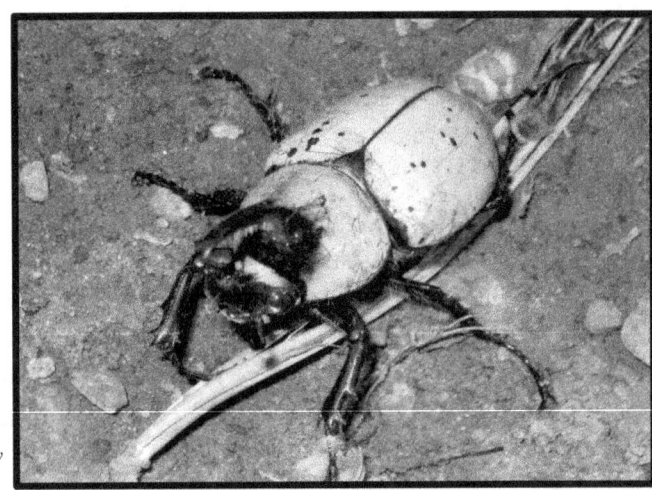

Courtesy of Emily Askew, '04 –
Photography Class – Northern Arizona University

9
Biographies/Autobiographies

Biographies are but the clothes and buttons of the man.
The biography of the man himself cannot be written.
Mark Twain

☛ *Students will use costumes, wigs and photos to assist in the writing of biographies and autobiographies.*

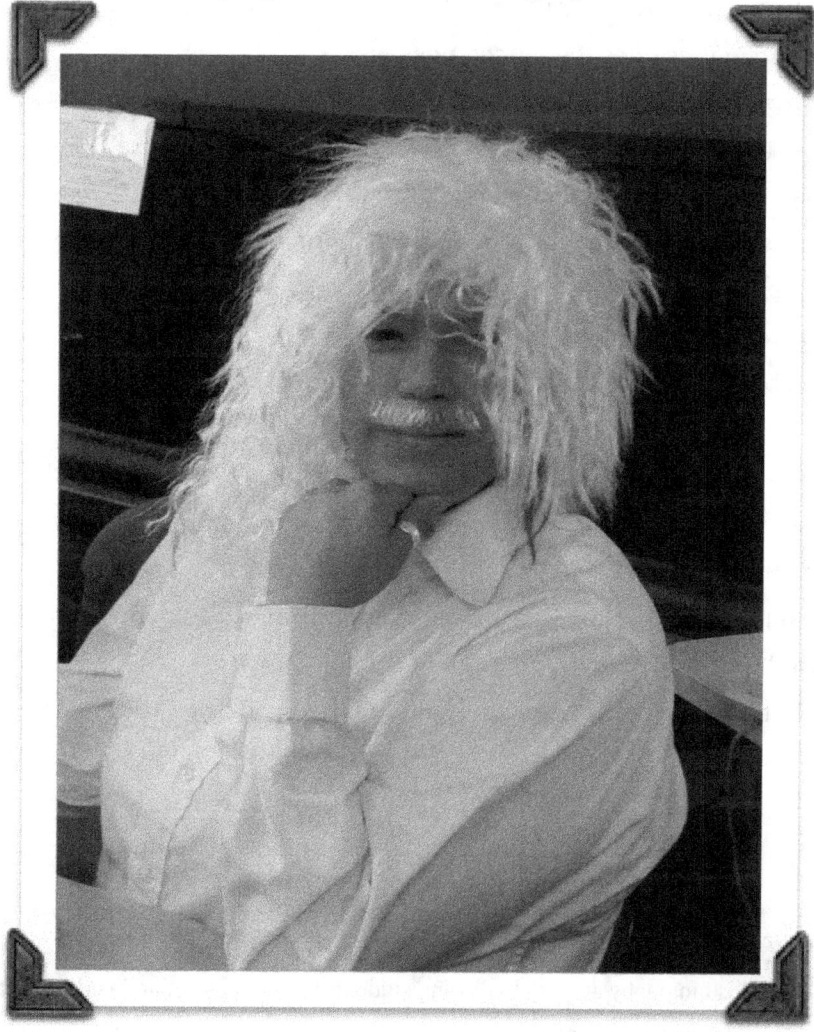

Student (Albert Einstein) in my Social Studies Class, Northern Arizona University

Here We Go!

❏ Show various biography books to students. Discuss the definition of a *biography* and *autobiography*.

❏ Place on the overhead the 6 elements of writing a good biography:

What is the name of the subject,

How old is the person,

Where does the person live,

What makes the person special or unique,

What admirable qualities does the person possess,

What has the person 'said' that tells about his or her mission or character.

❏ Students will use self-portraits. They will use another student's self-portrait to write a short biography, using the 6 elements of good biography writing.

❏ Students will select one of the four following options to write another biography: *a well-known American, a celebrity guest, a well-known person of the century or decade, or a leader in the news.*

❏ The fun part begins when each student will use wigs, costumes, etc., to dress as their chosen person, and have someone take a photo of them in that costume.

❏ They will research and write their one page biography and attach it to the photo.

❏ Each student will also create a journal entry written as the person whose biography they have written.

❏ They will listen to or read each other's biographies and discuss the elements of the biographies that were the most interesting to them.

❏ Show the photo on the previous page. Ask students who it is (Albert Einstein). The over-night assignment is to come back to class the following day with one interesting fact about Albert Einstein and use chart paper to display Einstein's photo and all the facts.

What Else Can We Do

✳ Wrap some fun in this biography activity by having students take a photo of an inanimate object either in the room, cafeteria, or on the playground.

✳ Students will use the 6 elements of biography writing to write a biography of the inanimate object.

✳ Or, have students *an object in the classroom* and write or tell the *life story* of it.

10
Biographies/Autobiographies Again

When writing a biography your real concern is what organization tells the best story
and teaches most effectively.
C.S. Wyatt

☞ *Students will use photos of nature's critters to create researched*
biographies, including one unique fact about the critter.

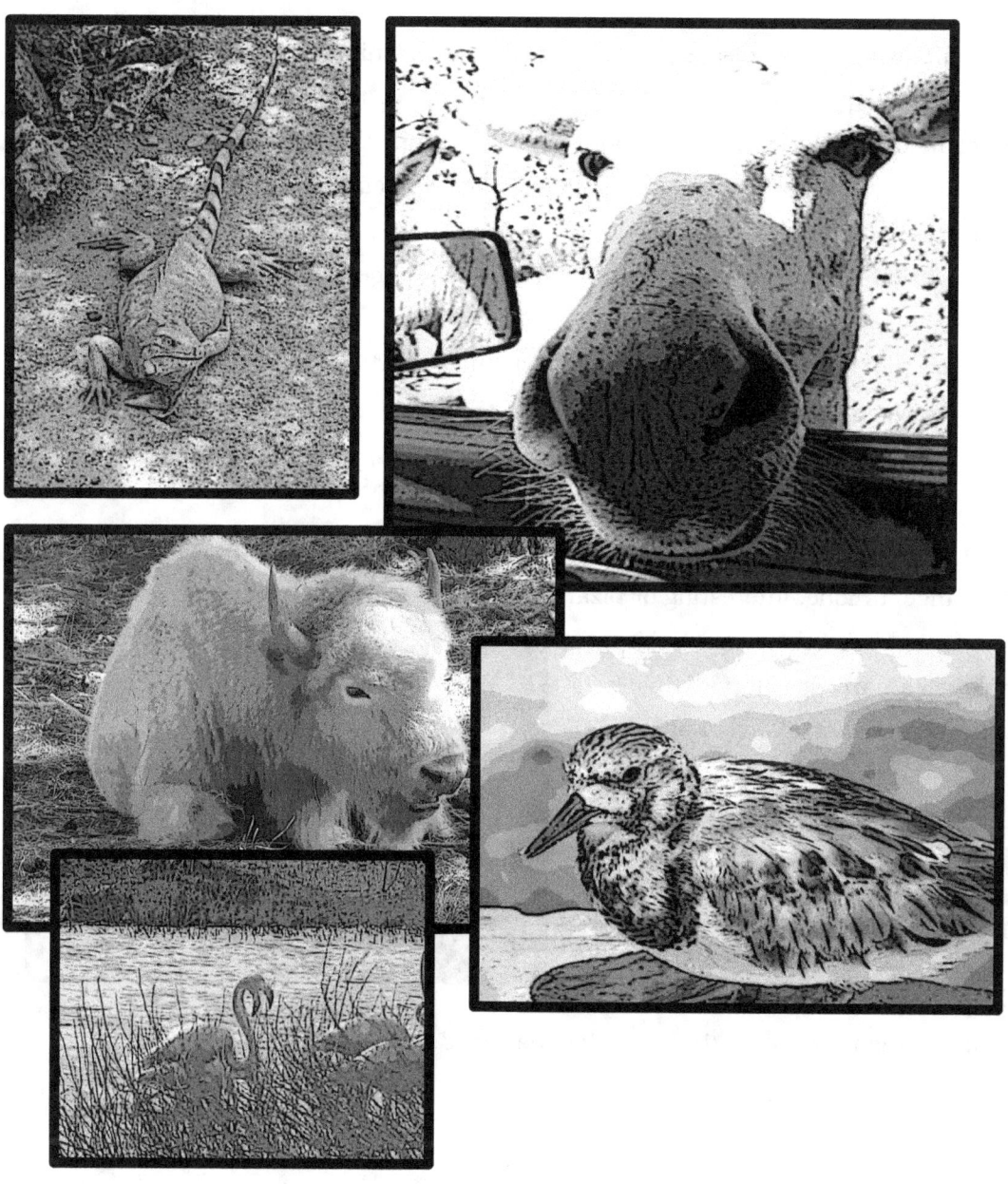

Here We Go!

❏Students will create a mystery script or story about their animal(s).

❏ Students will write a *fictional story about* their animal(s).

❏ Students will research and write 10 facts about their animal(s).

❏ 4 students will create puppets of their animals and write and perform a combined puppet script.

❏ Students will write a commercial that features their animal(s).

❏ On slips of paper in 3 baskets, the teacher will write 5 possibilities each, for these 3 story elements: *setting, time period,* and *situation.* Students will pick one slip from each basket and write a story incorporating those three elements in a story. The *character,* of course, *will* be one of their animals.

❏ Show various biography books to students. Discuss the definition of a *biography* and *autobiography.*

❏ Place on the overhead the 6 elements of writing a good biography: *what is the name of the subject, how old is the person, where does the person live, what*

What Else Can We Do

✳ What a great subject! An old boot from *who knows where.* Students will take a photo of a strange, unique, interesting or bizarre object, add a photo effect, and write their

own biographies of the strange object, or simple tell a narrative story of this ratty old boot with added charcoal photo effects.

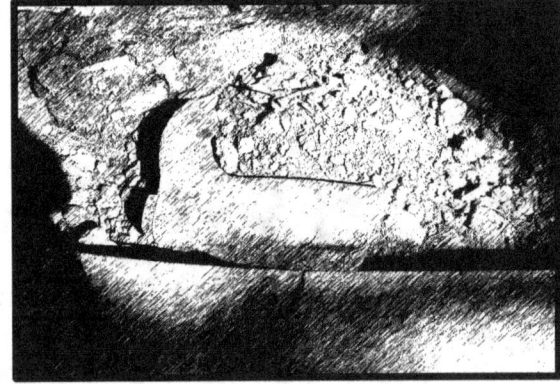

✳ Unrelated Object : For some students who need more intrigue with their writing, toss out of a photo of a totally unrelated object, like the boot.Students will include the 'boot' in their story or

find an ending to the story that includes the "boot".

11
Bizarre

Wherever we go, across the Pacific of Atlantic, we meet, not similarity so much
as 'the bizarre'. Things astonish us, when we travel, that surprise nobody else.
Miriam Beard

☛ *Students will demonstrate an understanding of the word bizarre and
use that word to influence a piece of writing from an interesting photo.*

A Bizarre Little Sighting in Kanab, Utah
Sometimes when we look from afar
The things that we see seem bizarre
But on closer inspection
We pause and we reckon
That some things in life aren't quite par
Take this plane in a truck if you can
What's the possible cause for this plan
Did the tires all go flat
Did the wings hit a bat
Did the cockpit get gritty with sand
It was simple, so simple, I found
When the pilot yelled out, with resound
That the gas for his truck
Was much cheaper, what luck
So he just flew around on the ground
Author

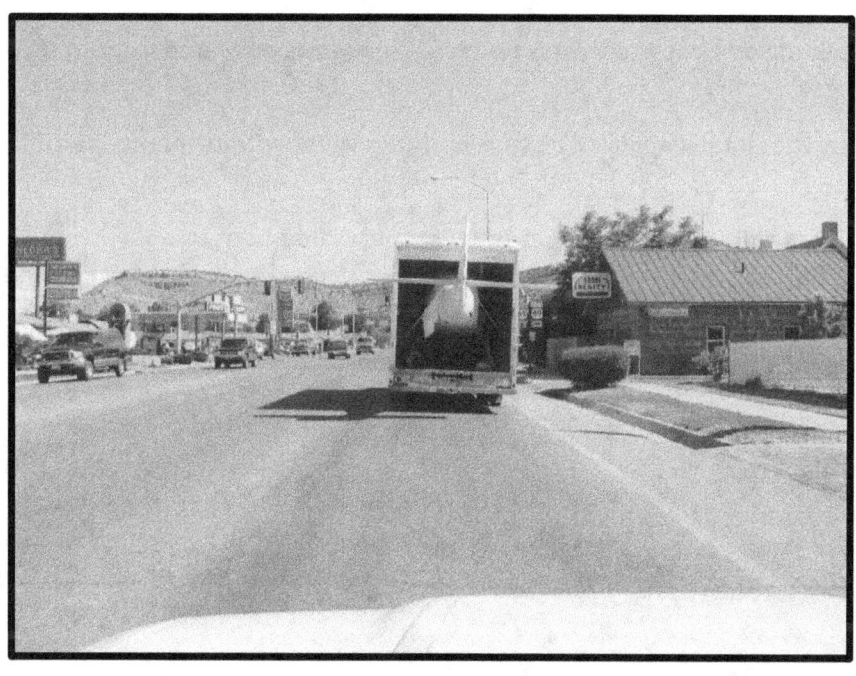

Here We Go!

❏As in most cases in this book, look at the previous photo and discuss it with the class.

❏ Beginning with the letter A, then B, etc., students will go around a say a sentence that applies to the photo of the plane in the truck.

❏ Define 'bizarre' and write synonyms of the word on the board. Discuss personal bizarre sightings the children have had, or biarre sitations that have occurred in their live.

❏ Read the poem about the photo. Ask for volunteers to write a 2 line rhyming poem about the photo.

❏ Some students will go to the Internet and find a Photo of the Year that may be bizarre.

❏ Some students will take a photo at school or home that appears to them to be bizarre.

❏ At a later time students will free write about their bizarre photo and add at least 4 synonyms of that word to the story.

❏ End with this relection journal entry: If everyday incuded one bizarre experience, I would like it/not like it because_____.

What Else Can We Do

✳Students will make a copy of the photo on the previous page and cut out only the truck and plane.

✳They will draw a landscape size picture and tape this cut out photo on a blank sheet of paper.

✳Other students will tell the new story they see or write about it.

✳Or they may use selected story titles such as these to help with their landscapes and stories: Jungle Landing, The Mystery of Flight 10, Stolen!, Island Ferry, Birthday Party

12
Black, White, & Color
(What's Worth Writing About)

Either write something worth reading, or do something worth writing.
Benjamin Franklin

☛ *Students will 'read' a photo, find what is worth writing about in the photo, color that one piece of the photo, then write a story that explains the photo, but emphasizes that colored piece.*

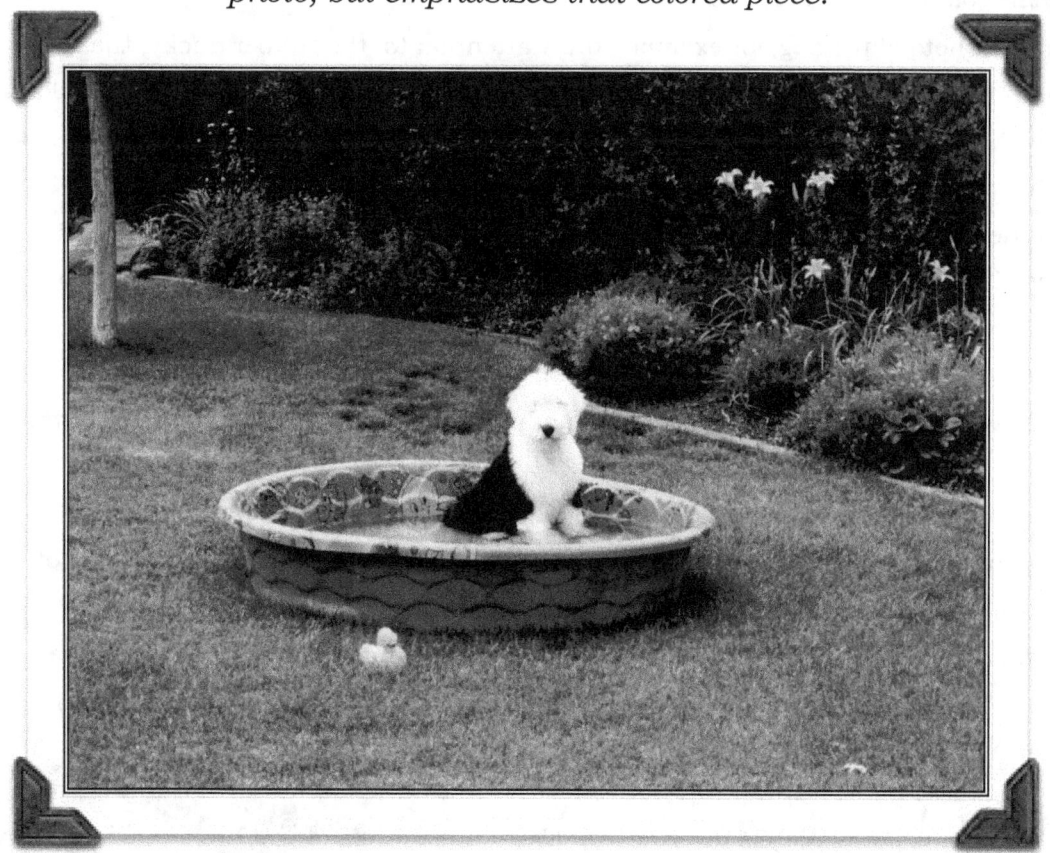

Bubba and his rubber ducky in the back yard doggie pool in Sedona, Arizona.

27

Here We Go

❏Look at the previous photo or have some photos in class that students can "read".

❏Look at the previous photo or have some photos in class that students can "read".

❏ Students will look at the photos and decide, individually, the part of the photo that is the most appealing to them in interest, in design, or in whatever realm they find a specific connection to their curiosity.

❏ In the photo of the dog, for example, draw attention to the rubber ducky, the rough spot in the grass, the one leaf on the grass, or even the water in the pool. Lead children to be observant and notice the small, somewhat hidden things that the photo reveals. Even *small things* are worth writing about.

❏ Students will make copies of the dog photo or their own photo, in black and white. They will select that ONE element of the photo that interests them in a strong way, and color it with map or colored pencils.

❏Students will write a story about the entire photo and bring in, specifically, and in a strong way, the colored part of the photo and its relevance to the overall theme of the story

❏ Students will have a class discussion of how they decided *what was worth writing about*not only when they looked at a photo but when they began the difficult task of narrowing down a writing idea so that it would be interesting to the reader.

❏ Now, read Benjamin Franklin's quote and lead a meaningful discussion on those words. Ask students WHY their piece is and was *worth writing about,* and even more importantly, was *worth reading*

What Else Can We Do

✻Here is a busy, busy photo of a garage sale. In it, students will find something *worth writing about,* without *naming the object.* After writing, each will put his writing piece in a pile and another student will randomly select someone else's paragraph. That student will *find* the object written about, and then color that object. Finally, that student will read the paragraph aloud and show the object.

13
Carvings

The character drives the story.

Unknown

☛ *Students will use tree carvings called arborglyphs to create various writing activities.*

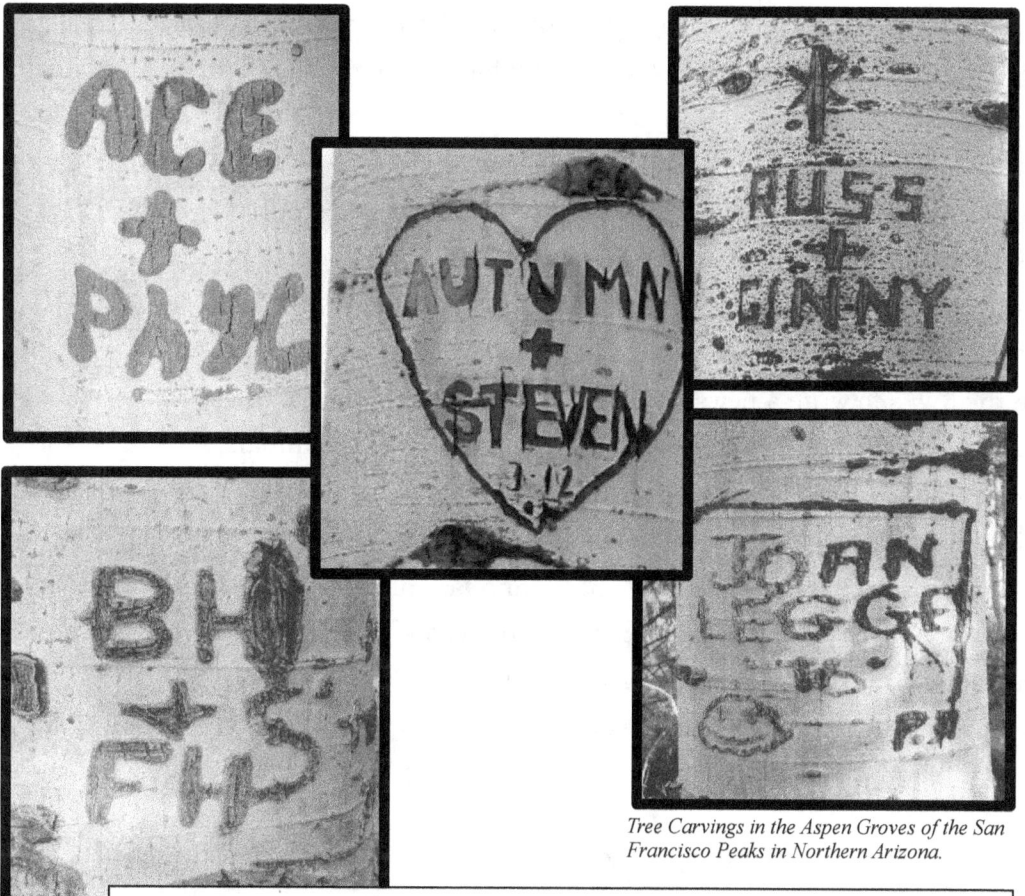

Tree Carvings in the Aspen Groves of the San Francisco Peaks in Northern Arizona.

Arborglyphs (Steve Nix, 2009) are carvings on trees that record names, dates, images, even poetry and prose. Beech, birch and aspen have traditionally been the trees of choice, preferred by most "artists". These species' smooth bark and light color makes a ready-made canvas for carving. Some consider arborglyphs to be a legitimate form of artistic expression and honor trees with these carvings. Others think it is just so much graffiti and another form of tree defacement. Most forest owners discourage the practice of carving on their trees.

Here We Go

❏Choose a carving and write about HOW two people in the carving met.

❏What were the colors of the sunset when the initials were carved into one of the trees? Use descriptive words.

❏ WHO is one of the carvers, in your imagination. Write his or her autobiography.

❏ Where have you noticed carvings in trees? What was the oldest? Write a story about that one.

❏ Choose a carving. What is the full name of that person? HOW did the parents choose that name?

❏ Write a story from the perspective of the tree being carved upon.

❏ Research tools used for carving onto a tree.

❏Write a 1st person story of how it may feel to be carved upon.

❏ Use the 5 W's to write a newspaper article about one of the carvings.

❏Create a bio sketch of someone WHO might have carved the initials.

❏ Write about the reason for carving initials into one of the trees.

❏ Write a 1st person point of view from the 'hands' that carved one of these initials or ❏ What does this saying mean?" A fool's name and face are aleays found in public places."

❏ If you were to carve something beside your name on a tree, what would it be and why?

❏ Write about why it is WRONG to carve on a tree. Back up your facts.

❏Write about why it is OKAY to carve on a tree. Back up your facts.

What Else Can We Do

✳ The character drives the story. While we may never know who carved each of the carvings, examine "Joe '97" and decide who you think the carver might have been.

 ✳ Develop a *persona map* for "Joe '97" by answering each of the following questions.

Name	Pets	Best Friend	Favorite Pasttime
Current Job	Favorite Foods	Collects	Hometown
Under the Bed	Favorite Saying	Birthplace	Pet
Peeves	Favorite Sport	Collects	Favorite
ClothingVacations	Best Friend	One Thing in His Pocket Education	

"Joe Smith"

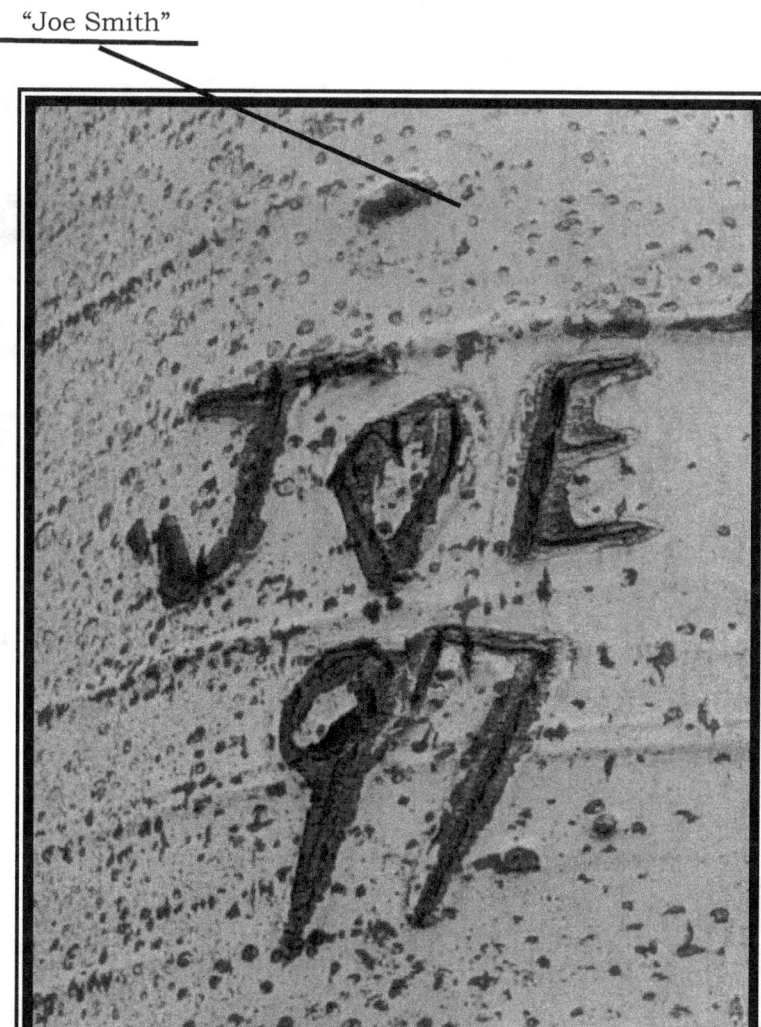

✳ Afterward, draw what you think "Joe 97" looks like.

14
Cinquains
Poetry is the rhythmical creation of beauty in words.
Edgar Allan Poe

☞ *Students will write Cinquains of 3 various styles, using original photos and art as stimulii.*

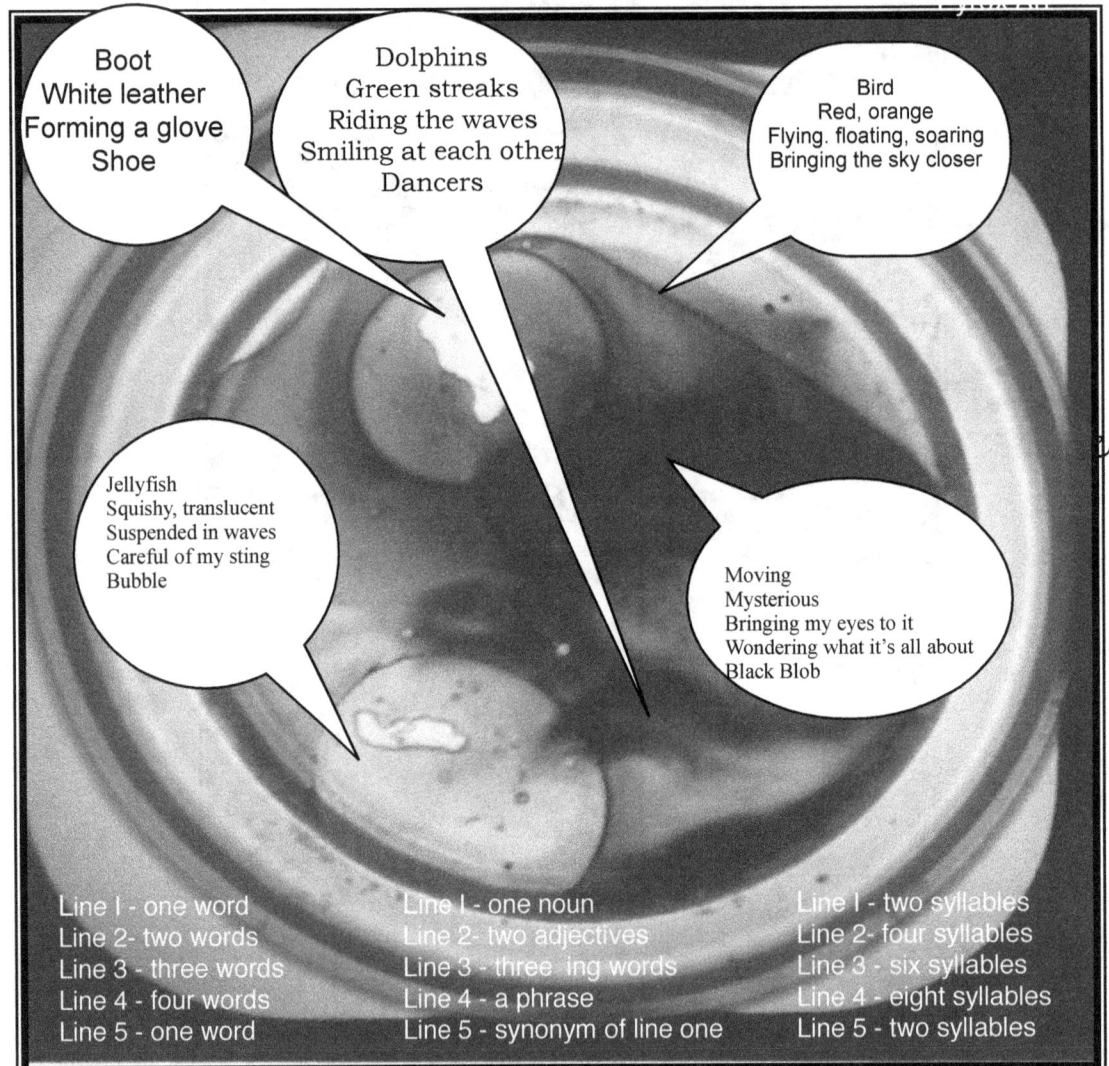

Boot
White leather
Forming a glove
Shoe

Dolphins
Green streaks
Riding the waves
Smiling at each other
Dancers

Bird
Red, orange
Flying. floating, soaring
Bringing the sky closer

Jellyfish
Squishy, translucent
Suspended in waves
Careful of my sting
Bubble

Moving
Mysterious
Bringing my eyes to it
Wondering what it's all about
Black Blob

Line 1 - one word	Line 1 - one noun	Line 1 - two syllables
Line 2- two words	Line 2- two adjectives	Line 2- four syllables
Line 3 - three words	Line 3 - three ing words	Line 3 - six syllables
Line 4 - four words	Line 4 - a phrase	Line 4 - eight syllables
Line 5 - one word	Line 5 - synonym of line one	Line 5 - two syllables

Place a Pyrex bowl on the overhead. Fill the bowl with a cup of water. To the water add a half-cup of vegetable oil. To that mixture, add one drop each of the 4 colors in a food coloring set. DO NOT STIR. Let the heat from the overhead create and change the colored form that presents itself in the Pyrex bowl. Use this as the focus for original cinquain writing pieces, using one of the above styles.

Here We Go

❏ The teacher will use the pyrex art and add only one color to the oil/water mixture.

❏ Students will, one at a time, write the name of an object they see in bowl on the board. No object can be duplicated, so adjectives must be used to decipher the different objects.

❏ Students will use the one object they and write a cinquain about it.

❏ Students will not use the REAL NAME of the object in their cinquains, rather synonyms of the object.

What Else Can We Do

✳ Upside Down Image - Use this upside down image of a lake scene to write a cinquain, then turn the image right side up and write another cinquain . To be even wilder, turn the image a quarter turn and you have yet another image to use as a stimulus for writing another cinquain.

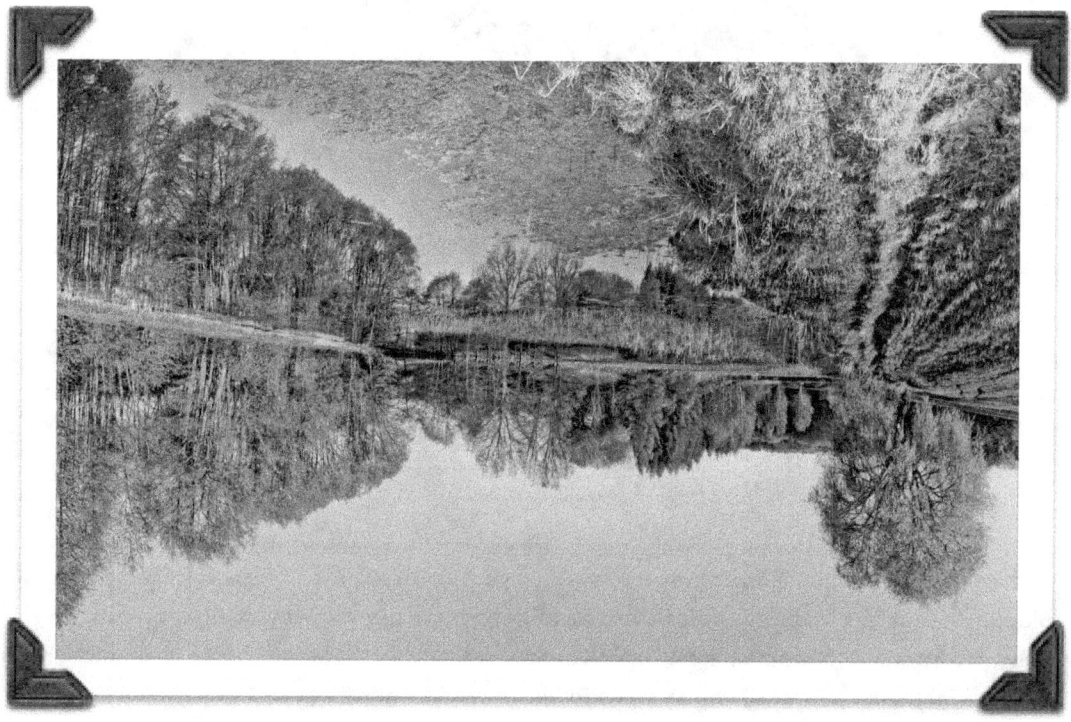

15
Cloze Technique
Teaching reading **IS** rocket science.
Louisa Moats

☛ *Students will demonstrate an understanding of the Cloze vocabulary strategy by writing stories from original photos, leaving blanks in these stories.*

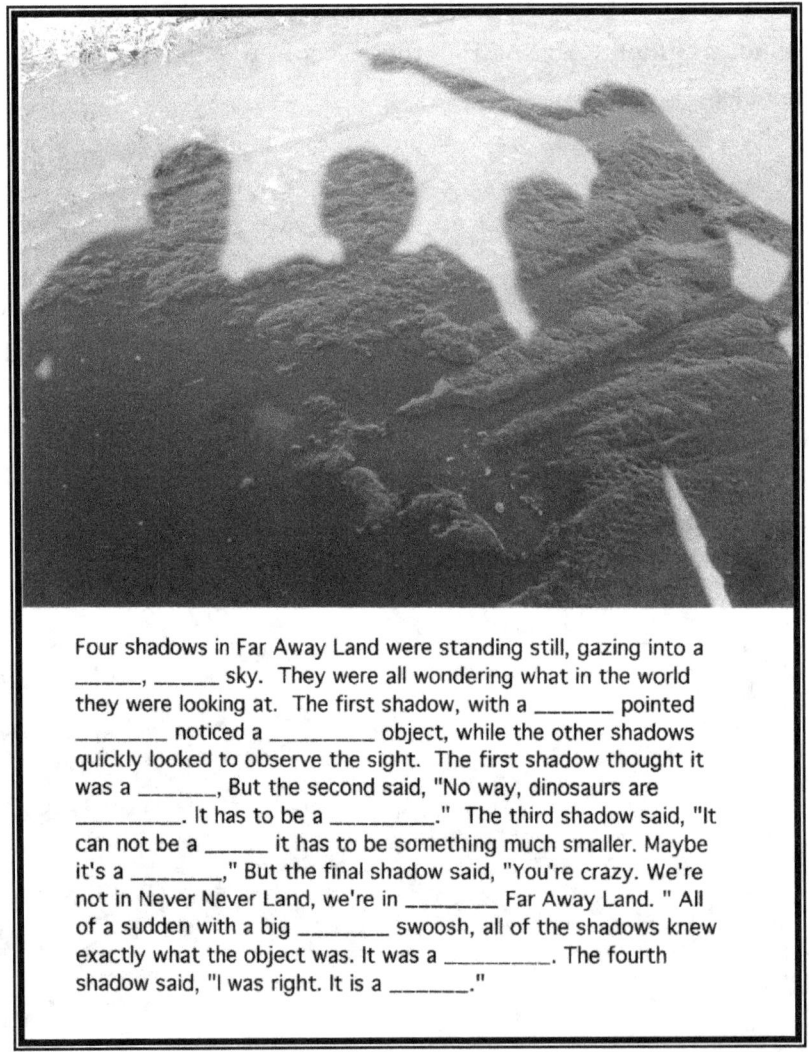

Four shadows in Far Away Land were standing still, gazing into a _____, _____ sky. They were all wondering what in the world they were looking at. The first shadow, with a _____ pointed _____ noticed a _____ object, while the other shadows quickly looked to observe the sight. The first shadow thought it was a _____, But the second said, "No way, dinosaurs are _____. It has to be a _____." The third shadow said, "It can not be a _____ it has to be something much smaller. Maybe it's a _____," But the final shadow said, "You're crazy. We're not in Never Never Land, we're in _____ Far Away Land. " All of a sudden with a big _____ swoosh, all of the shadows knew exactly what the object was. It was a _____. The fourth shadow said, "I was right. It is a _____."

A cloze is a comprehension and/or vocabulary strategy. Type a story leaving blanks. The blanks should be vocabulary words, nouns or describers like adjectives. After reading the story several times (administer cloze), the students fill in the blanks. Students should read on their own and use context clues to figure out the missing words.

A cloze should have 20-25 blanks. It should also be done several times through the year.

Here We Go

❏ Give students a generic photo such as the one on the previous page. Have them complete the story by filling in the blanks.

❏ Now make a copy a photo similar to the one below. Have students *add other cut out pictures* onto that photo (see *cat*fish, *monkey*fish *dog*fish, *Iguana*fish *happy*fish).

❏ Students will write their own stories, leaving 10 blanks so other students can read and fill in the blanks according to what works for them.

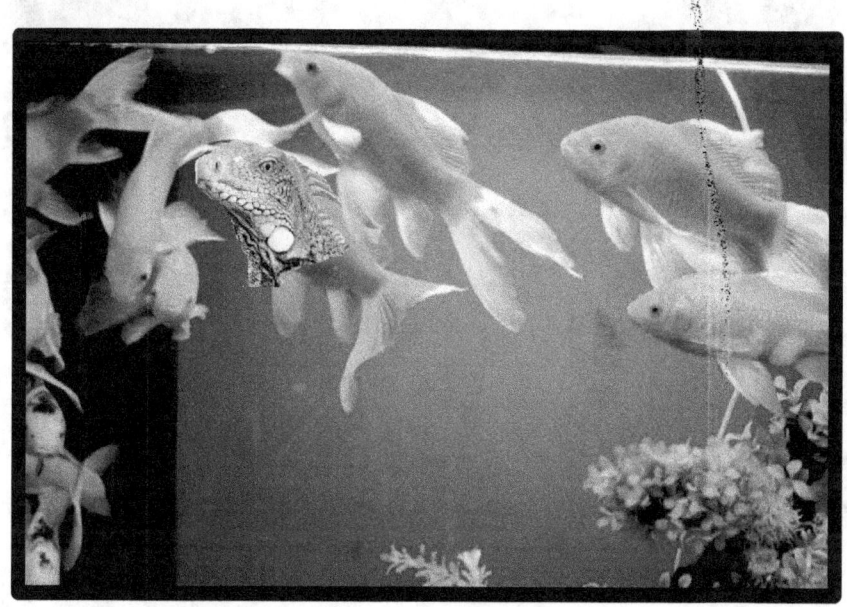

What Else Can We Do

✱   On the board write these directions: 2 Nouns, 2 verbs, 3 adjectives, 1 adverb, 1 pronoun. Groups will write a story using these parts of speech. Another group will take a photo that describes the story.

Starter Words

swim	warm	hide	seek	rocks
reef	gills	friends	deep	sun
places	nook	food	glistened	water
name	bubbles	down	clown	tummy
ocean	blue	clear	fast	hidden

16
Coming and Going with Emotions
The first and simplest emotion which we discover in the human mind is curiosity.
Edmund Burke

Students will use photos to discuss and write stories incorporating various emotions.

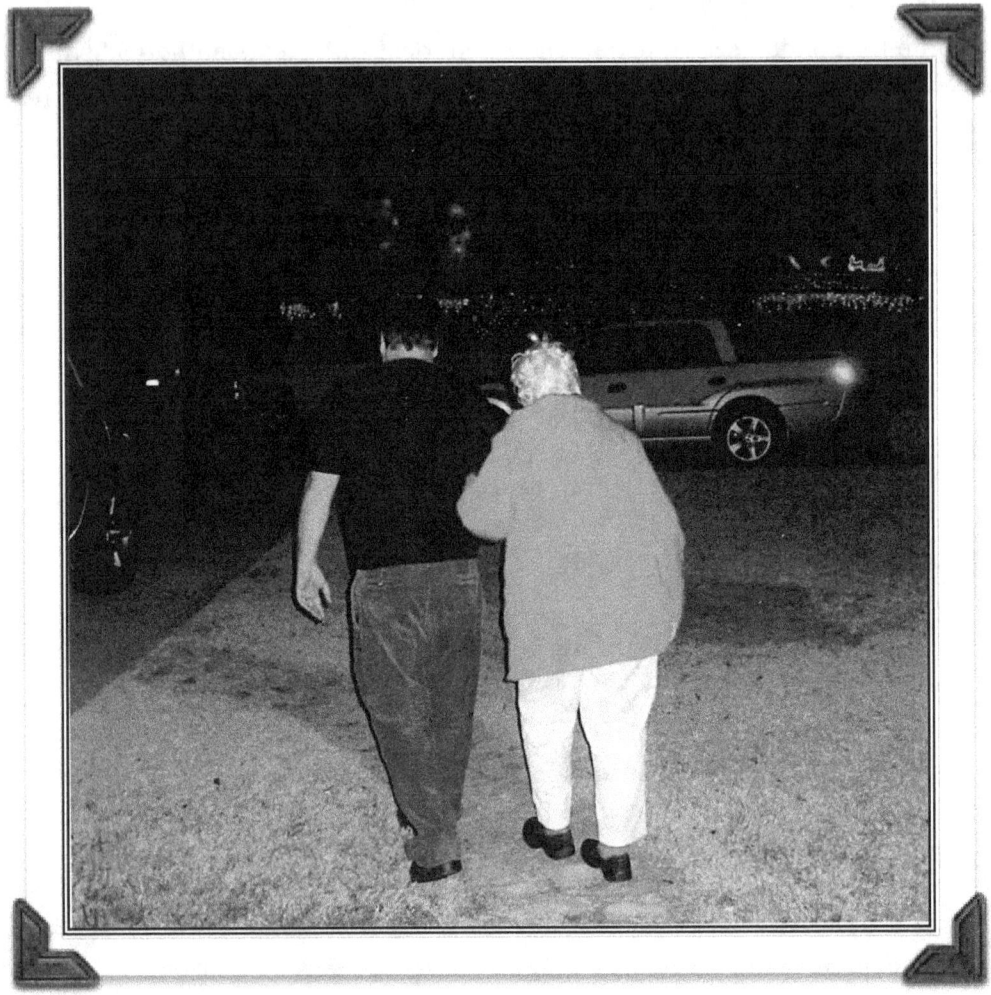

The old woman, wrapped in the red jacket of a youth she could not remember held
on to the young man as he created the steps to the car for both of them. Earlier,
surrounded by family and the glitter of party lights, the old woman laughed at everything,
and nothing. There were moments when the far off look in her eyes revealed a destination
that none in the room had ever taken. She ate as if she had never tasted food before, and
cradled the stuffed animals given to her, furry reminders of a time long erased from her
Swiss cheese mind.

Zestful

When the two finally got into the car, the old woman started chattering non-stop. She told the young man about the bridge that had to be crossed in order to get to her house when she was a child. She told him about how her father lost a finger while grinding corn in the barn, and how he wiggled the 'nub' at dinner every night to make her laugh.

When they arrived, the young man helped her inside the residence. She hugged him confidently and then began to walk down the hall. "Have a good evening', he yelled after her. "I will', she called back. "I'm going to pick plums".

Helpless

When the young man helped the old woman into the car for the long drive to the Assisted Living Community where she lived, she asked where they were going. He told her that he was taking her home. She looked into his eyes and simply said,' Where is that"? He tried to explain what 'home' was to her, but she turned her head and stared out the window. "The plum tree is full', she spoke, in a voice that sounded like clouds. He continued to drive

Impatience

As they drove to the retirement residence, the young man could tell that the old woman was anxious to get to their destination. "Are we almost there?" she asked a dozen times. "How much farther?" she repeated over and over.

When they pulled up to the parking space, the old woman tried to open the door before the car had come to a full stop. "What's your hurry?' the young man said as he held her in her seat. "I've got to get them before any one else", she snapped, fumbling for the door handle.

"Get what", he asked with a surprised look. She stared at the young man with half closed eyes, and then shook her head as if she could bear no more. "The plums', she spat, and rattled the door handle to get the point across.

Here We Go

❏ Show several photos plus the one on the previous page. Discuss the *feelings* portrayed in these photos. Put a list of 10 diverse feelings on the board. Discuss various definitions. Show *one photo*. Ask students to use several of the new feeling words to create different endings that may come to mind.

❏ One selected student will take a photo that includes people in the shot. One selected student in the class will use that photo to *write a narrative* on the same sheet as the photo, which will then be displayed on a bulletin board.

❏ Other students will select 3 feeling words from the list in which to write *3 different endings* to the photo story that is on the bulletin board. (See previous page.)

❏ Students will read some of their endings and pick one they seem to like the best. They will explain the reason for their selection, using the photo as part of their rationale.

❏ All of the endings will be placed around the central photo. Students will randomly read endings and *reflect upon* how particular emotions can make a photo seem totally different from what is initially seen.

What Else Can We Do

✳ Take a *group shot* of the class. Students will select classmates in the photo other than themselves. They will choose a different emotion to write an ending to a paragraph that relates to one of the students in the class. Or they can use a photo of a class in past times and do the same assignment.

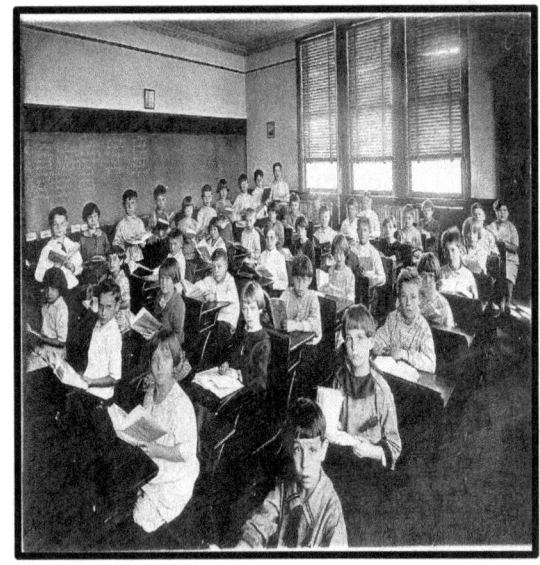

17
Cut and Paste
If everyone is thinking alike, then somebody isn't thinking.
George S. Patton

☛ *Students will cut & paste items onto a landscape or portrait photo and write or tell about the new photo .*

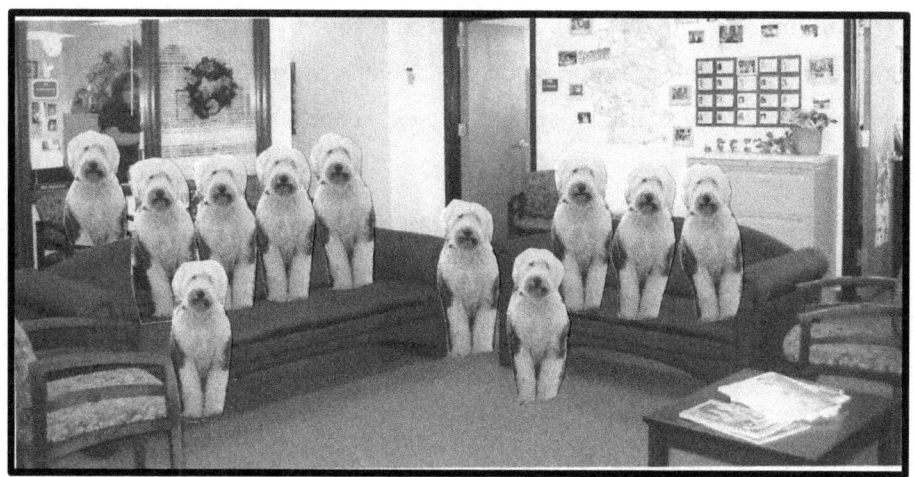

Photography Assignment Examples, Northern Arizona University Photography/Writing Class

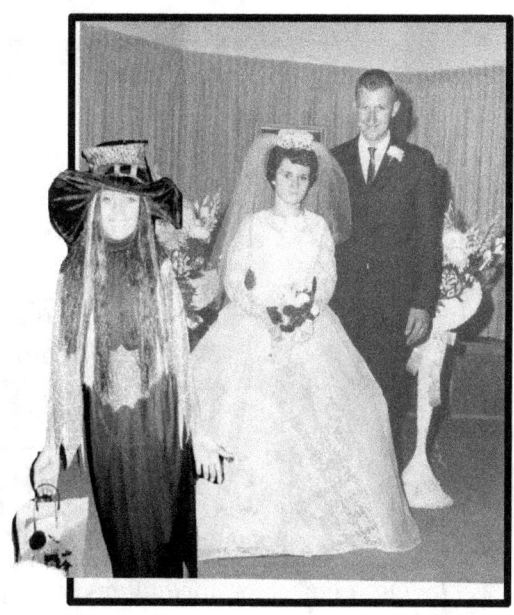

Here We Go

❑ Show art examples from the book, *Rene Magritte: Now You See It, Now You Don't,* by Angela Wenzel. Some of the art examples are not appropriate for children, so be alert. Lead a discussion on *imagination.*

❑ Students will look at the photos from the previous page and discuss the differences between imagination and truth that can be found in those photos.

❑ Now look at one of previous photos again and: *tell its story, ask 3 questions about it, create an add-on story from it, use the photo to 'sell' something, describe all of the parts of the imagined photo.*

❑ Students will shoot a generic photo or one from the teacher's files. Each student will get a copy (on card stock) of that photo.

❑ Students will DRAW or apply cutouts that represents one object, character, or such, right on the photo.

❑ Students will swap photos so that another student will write one paragraph of the imagined moment that the photo represents.

❑ Students will once again discuss the difference between imagination and truth.

What Else Can We Do

*Teacher will create an imagined moment photo with cutouts, or drawings, and write a prompt for each student to complete.

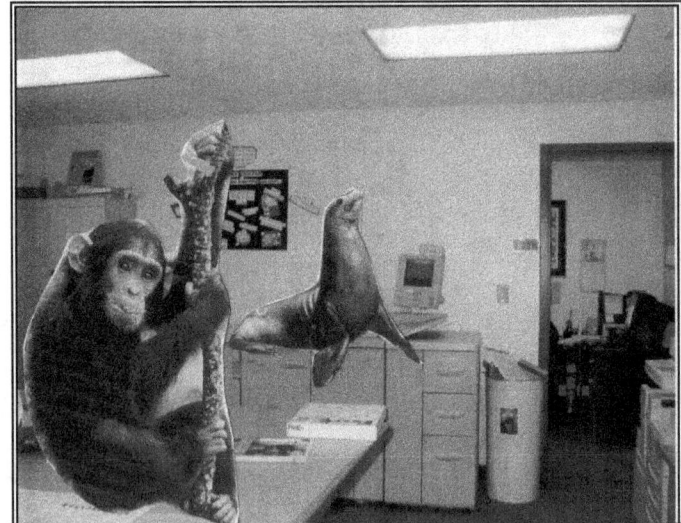

On a perfectly normal day, in a perfectly normal office, inside a perfectly normal building, something very strange began to happen. And it wasn't perfectly normal at all.

18
Dialogue

Dialogue is the most effective way of resolving conflict.

Tenzin Gyatso, The 14th Dalai Lama

☞ *Students will use photos to create, write, and act out four-person dialogues.*

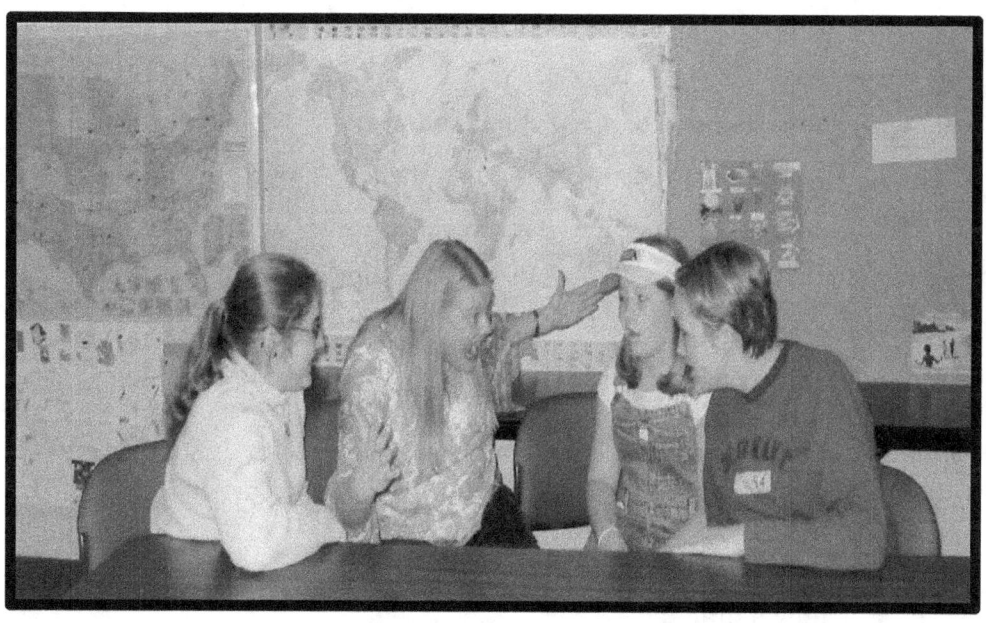

Yvonne   Linda   Megan   Cami

Linda: *I had a hot dog for dinner last night and it was 3 feet long.*

Megan: *I went to the same restaurant and had the same kind of hot dog, and boy am I sick.*

Cami: *Which restaurant?*

Yvonne: *This sounds better than the hamburger I had.*

Cami: *Please, please, please don't tell that story again.*

Yvonne: *Oh, do. I think it is so funny. Wait till you hear it.*

Linda: *Well, it goes like this. On my way to school today I tripped over a worm that was stretched on the ground, and it was this long.*

Megan: *I think you tripped and fell on your head instead.*

Megan: *I've got a toothache.*

Yvonne: *I'm glad it's you and not me.*

Linda: *Do you know that a root on a tooth can be this long?*

Cami: *Where did you hear*

Here We Go

❏ Students will get into groups of four.

❏ Students will create various creative body and/or facial expressions.

❏ Shoot random shots of each group and their creative expressions. Locale of shots can be each group's choice.

❏ Use real names for each group or give fictional names.

❏ Students will write 3 different dialogues among the four group members depending on the creative body and facial expression that are observed.

❏ Now try to act selected conversations out in pantomime.

＊ Find a photo with animals. These 6 cows may be spectators to something. Use the following events and ask students to create dialogues from the 6 cows about:

1. Seeing a tornado

2. Watching a drag race

3. Waiting to be fed

4. Seeing a truck drive up

5. Watching their baby calves

6. Other

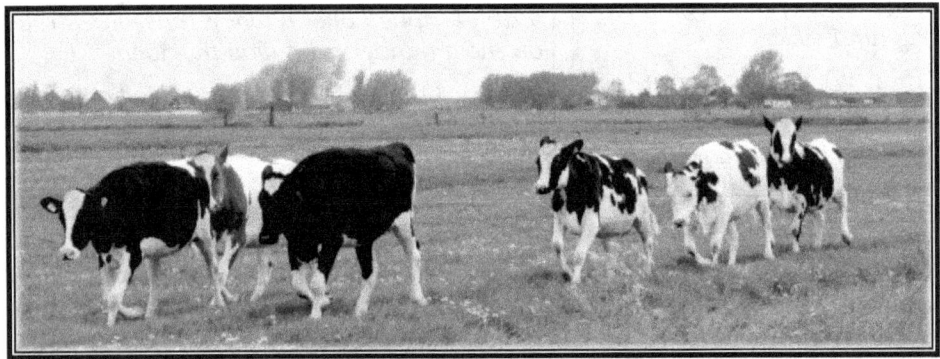

19
Doors
Beauty is a door to the soul.

Anonymous

☛ *Students will discuss the 5 elements of photography and apply them to the door photos.*

☛ *Students will take photos of doors and use them to write or tell stories about what is on 'the other side'.*

Essential Elements of Photography

1. **Composition**- Move in closer to your subject and decide what part of the photo you want your 'reader' to pay attention to. Take your time before you shoot.

2. **Exposure** – Pay attention so that your photo isn't too dark, too light, too heavily shadowed, too sun washed. Take your time before you shoot.

3. **Feelings** – Make sure your photo evokes some kind of feeling. What feelings do YOU have when you look through the lens at your shot?

4. **Tell a Story** – Before you snap the photo, look through the lens to see if there is, indeed, a story waiting to be told in your picture. Think it through before you shoot.

5. **Life** - Take photos that simply *say something about life.* Are you bringing something *real* to your reader?

Think it through before you shoot.

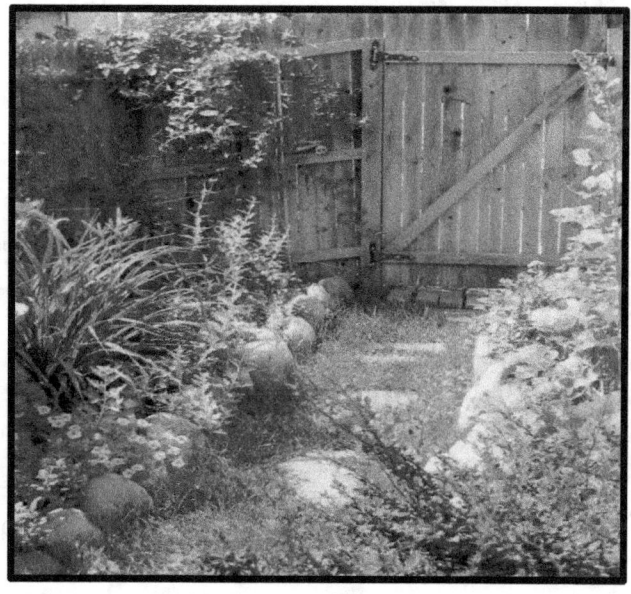

Here We Go

❏ Show several examples of <u>doors.</u> Students will brainstorm or discuss where these doors may lead.

❏ Show the photos again and have students think of sentences that would 'fit' the doors. These sentences can be symbolic, abstract in nature, figurative, literal, and so on.

❏ Show one photo such as the garden on the previous page. Make one copy of that photo on regular cardstock or plain paper. Send it around the room. Students will write one sentence that 'fits' that photo, focusing on the door.

❏ Share those sentences with each other and discuss the various connections the door has to the students.

❏ Teacher will lead a discussion of the 5 elements of photography and use the photo of the garden to dissect the photo into the 5 elements.

❏ Students will write a reflective piece using one of the following words as it applies to the garden photo: composition, exposure, feelings, stories, and life.

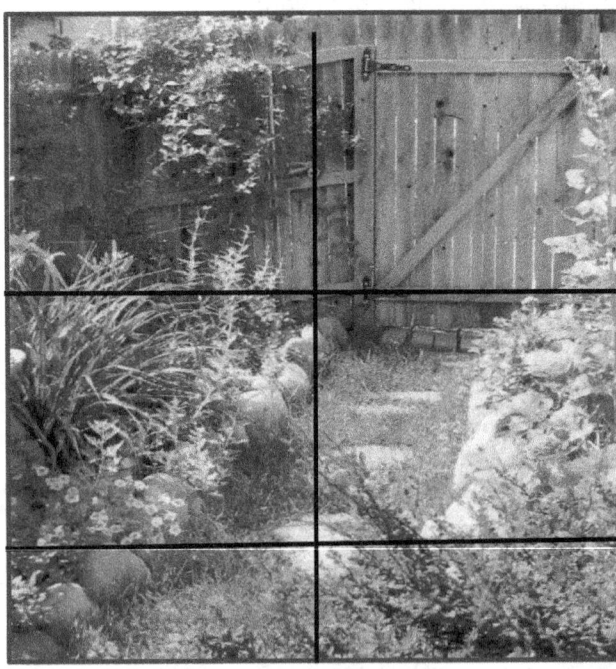

What Else Can We Do

✳ Choose a photo and crisscross it with thin straight lines these. Squares need not be the same size. Now write a paragraph about what you see in the photo where the lines converge. This exercise helps children with observation skills, and assists them in the ability to *see* photo correctly.

20
Endings and Beginnings

There will come a <u>time</u> when you believe everything is finished.
That will be the beginning.
Louis L'Amour

☛ *Students will use photos to tell and write stories that include original beginnings, middles, and ends.*

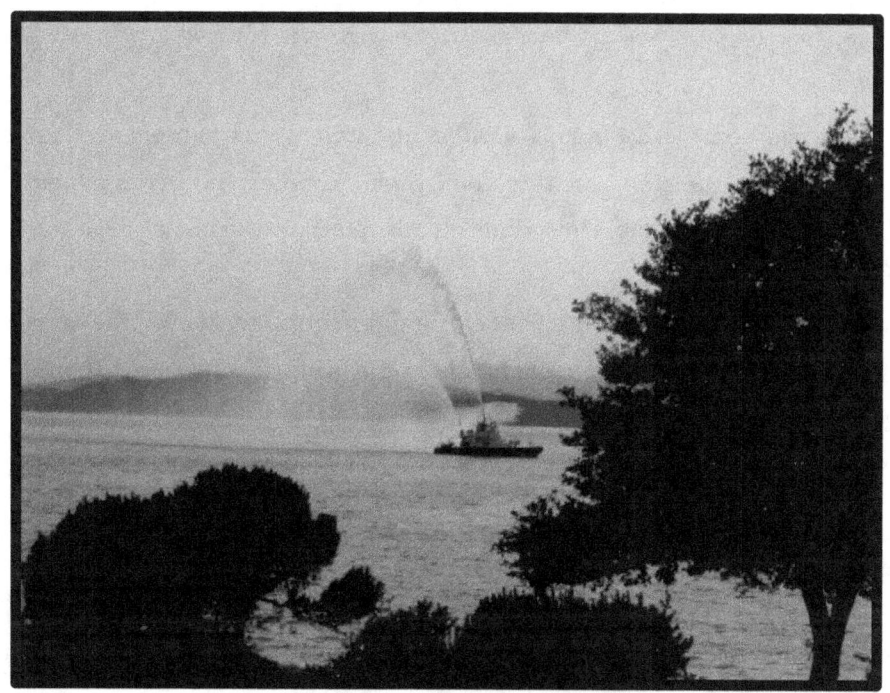

Look at this photo. Share 2 original Endings (factual and fictitious), with another student, of what happens immediately after the fireboat goes **past the trees.**

Look at this photo. Share 2 original Beginnings (factual and fictitious), with another student, of what happens as the fireboat **comes into view from the left** of the

Look at this photo. Share 2 events (factual and fictitious), with another student, that **occurred on the fireboat itself,** after the beginning of the story and before the

Here We Go

❏ Read this short paragraph to students and lead a discussion on personal experiences that the paragraph evokes.

The wind began to howl like a thousand coyotes as the trees twisted their leaves and branches in an effort to hide from the dangerous gusts. The two children looked at the tall, bending boughs and ran for cover in a nearby cave. "Whew, that was scary," they screamed over the noise, while they sat in the dark, mysterious place, waiting out the storm.

❏ Lead a discussion on the *beginning, middle,* and *end* of this paragraph. Pick out words that strengthen the story such as *howl, gusts, coyotes, dangerous, bending, cave, screamed, dark, mysterious,* etc. Have children swap other words for these that might enhance the story even more.

❏ Students, in groups, will create and take original shots that depict this scenario of the cave. They will add something to the shot that could possibly create a different beginning, middle or end.

What Else Can We Do

*Students in groups of 3 will choose 3 objects in a photo taken from one of the group member's houses. Rotate the three objects, as beginning, middle, and end pieces and each group member will write a different paragraph/story using the three objects in different order (Ex. guitar, stool, TV, plant).

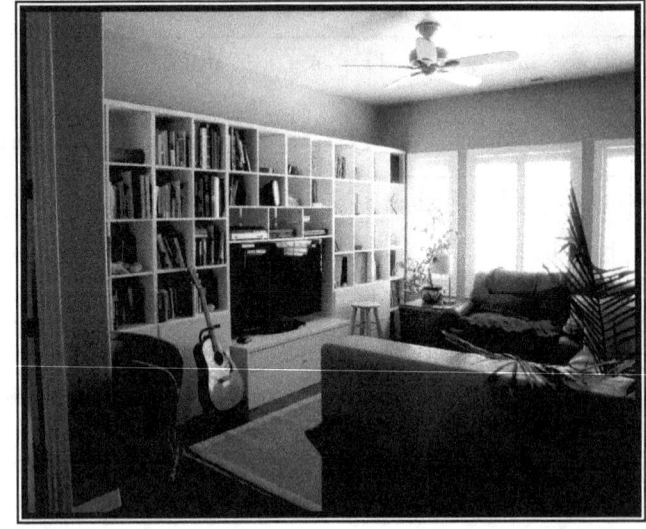

21
Expository Text

Be nice to nerds. Chances are you'll end up working for one.
Bill Gates

☛ *Students will design and create original machines and write expository texts relating to the machines.*

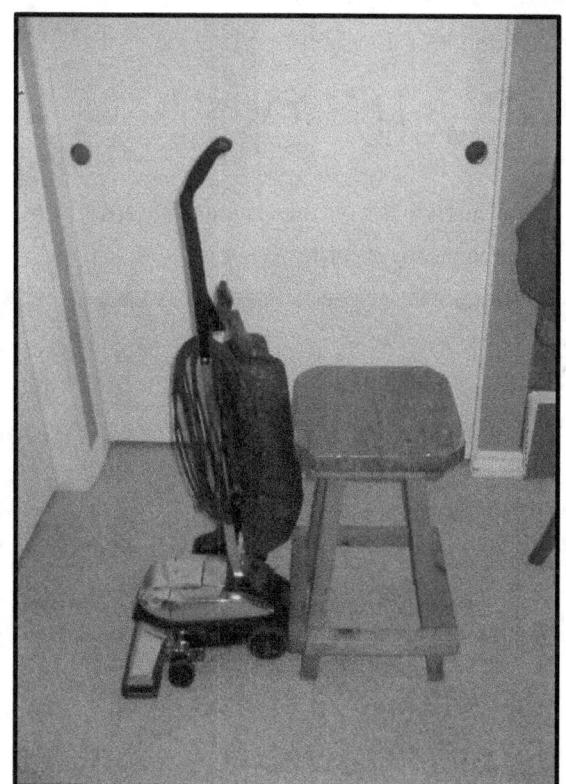

Riding Vacuum Cleaner

It is:
Quiet
Simple to Operate
Uses no Gas
Stores Easily
Comfortable
and
Lets you hold your kitty
in
your lap as you vacuum
the
cat hair away!

Get Your
Riding Vacuum Cleaner
TODAY
$149.99

You'll love what it does
for your floors
AND
your arthritis!!!

Unlike narrative texts which are written from the author's imagination, *expository* writing is a type of writing where the purpose is to inform, explain, describe, or define the author's subject to the reader.

The creator of an *expository text* cannot assume that the reader or listener has prior knowledge or prior understanding of the topic that is being discussed.

47

Here We Go

❏ Engage in discussions regarding expository writing and reading.

❏ Look at models of expository writing.

❏ Design and create original machines that make life easier for the user.

❏ Take photos of the original machines.

❏ Write expository text : to *sell* the product, to *describe* the product, to *give testimony* to the product, to *compare* the product, and to *describe pros and cons* of the product.

What Else Can We Do

✻ Old photos are incredibly fun to collect and use. Students will use old photos found at garage sales, junk stores, and antique stores as stimuli for the following prompts for expository writing.

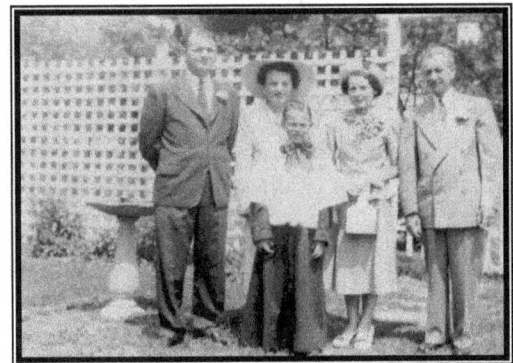 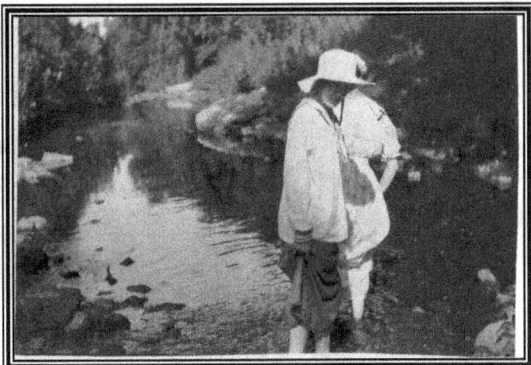

The Best Day I Ever Spent With My Family

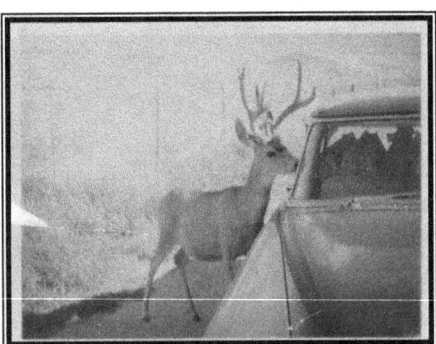 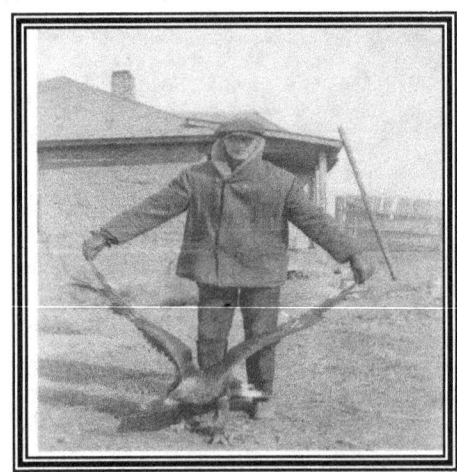

How To Take Care Of A Wild Animal

22

Feelings/Emotions

We apply law to facts. We don't apply feelings to facts.
Sonya Sotomayor

☞ *Students will shoot shots that represent needs met and needs not met and write accordingly.*

absorbed adventurous affectionate alert alive amazed amused animated appreciative ardent aroused astonished balanced blissful breathless buoyant calm carefree cheerful comfortable complacent composed concerned confident content cool curious dazzled delighted delirious eager ebullient ecstatic effervescent elated enchanted encouraged

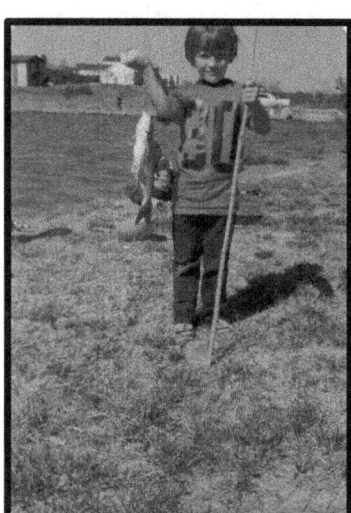

energetic engrossed enlivened enthusiastic excited exhilarated expansive expectant exultant fascinated free friendly fulfilled glad gleeful glorious glowing good-humored grateful gratified happy helpful hopeful inquisitive inspired intense interested intrigued invigorated involved joyous joyful jubilant keyed-up kind lovely loving lucky mellow merry mirthful moved optimistic overjoyed overwhelmed peaceful perky playful pleasant pleased powerful proud quiet radiant rapturous refreshed regenerated rejuvenated relaxed relieved safe satisfied secure sensitive serene special spellbound splendid stimulated surprised sympathetic tender thankful thrilled touched tranquil trusting unique upbeat vivacious warm wide-awake wonderful zestful

> **Needs Met**

afraid aggravated agitated alarmed aloof angry anguished annoyed anxious apathetic apprehensive aroused ashamed awful badly beat bewildered bitter blah blue bored brokenhearted burned out cautious chagrined cold concerned confused cool cross defiant defensive dejected depressed despairing despondent desperate detached disaffected disenchanted disappointed discouraged disgruntled disgusted disheartened dismayed displeased disquieted distant distressed disturbed downcast downhearted dull edgy embarrassed embittered empty exasperated exhausted fatigued fearful fidgety foolish forlorn frightened frustrated furious gloomy grouchy guilty harried heavy helpless hesitant horrified horrible hostile hot humdrum, hurt impatient impotent indifferent insecure insignificant intense intolerant introverted irate irked irritable irritated jealous jittery keyed-up lazy leery lethargic listless lonely lost lousy ludicrous mad mean melancholy miserable misunderstood mopey morose mournful naughty nauseated needy nervous nettled numb obsessed obnoxious overwhelmed panicky passive pathetic perplexed pessimistic powerless puzzled rancorous rebellious reluctant remorseful repelled resentful resigned restless sad scared

sensitive shaky shocked silly skeptical sleepy sneaky sorrowful sorry spacey spiritless startled stubborn stupid sullen surprised suspicious tense tepid terrible terrified tired torn trapped troubled uncomfortable unconcerned uneasy unglued unhappy unimportant unnerved unsteady upset uptight useless used vacuous vehement vexed vicious violated violent vulnerable weary wistful withdrawn woeful worried worthless wretched

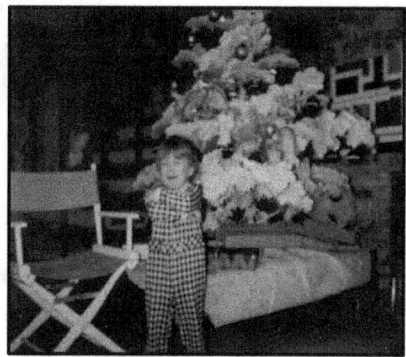

> **Needs Unmet**

49

Here We Go!

❏ Students will select one emotion word that is not part of their vocabulary in both the Needs Met column and the Needs Unmet column on the previous page.

❏ Shoot two photos that represent those particular feelings or emotion words. Make sure these are honest photos, not staged.

❏ Write personal episodes of having those particular feelings or emotions. Discuss why those particular emotion words chosen were the 'right' words for each personal story.

❏ During the week, practice using those new vocabulary words in appropriate ways.

What Else Can We Do

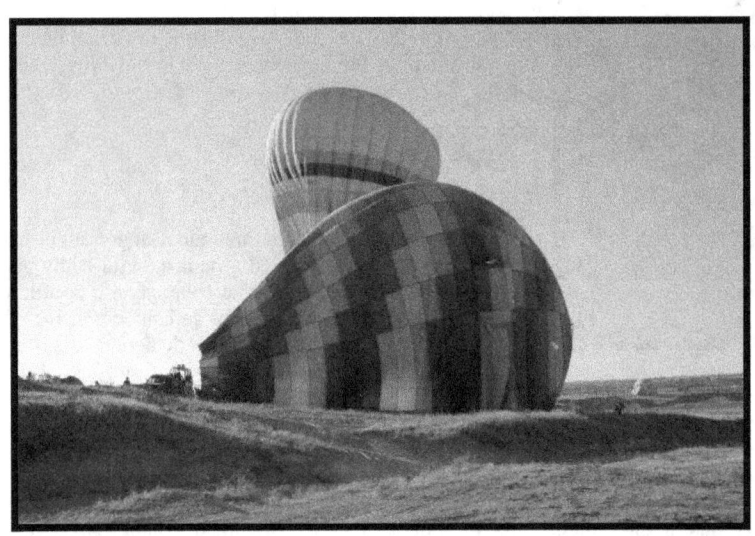

✳ Pick 5 emotions from the previous page and tell about the emotions as they applies to the photo of the balloons. Using any writing format to put that emotion into words.

✳ Select one emotion that embraces this photo <u>or a personal vacation photo</u>. Write a simile or metaphor that captures the chosen emotion and the photo.

✳Write an emotion focused story from the point of view of the young boy <u>or a vacation photo</u> as it relates to your (a) first visit to the Balloon Fest or personal vacation site, (b) your 5th visit to the Balloon Fest or personal vacation site or (c) your visit to the Balloon Fest or vacation site ***instead*** of going to Disneyland.

23
Five W's +1

(Who, When, What, Where ,Why, & How)
I keep six honest serving men (They taught me all I knew)
Their names are What and Why And When
And Where and How and Who
Rudyard Kipling

☞ Students will use the 5 W's +1 to write newspaper articles, authentic and non fiction, which include appropriate   photos.

The Daily Eye

Here We Go!

❑ Cut out several age appropriate articles from newspapers. As students to listen for the *who, what, when, where, why & how* of one of the articles being read. Discuss the photo on the previous page and the W's that might accompany that photo.

❑ In groups, students will take another article and brainstorm the 5+1 W's. The information will be underlined and shared with the rest of the class.

❑ Show several photos to the students. Brainstorm article topics arising from the photos. Discuss the 5+1 W's that could be used in the photo/article.

❑ Students will then find one article in the next day's paper and create and shoot a photo that would represent that particular article, then, using the W's, rewrite the article in their own words. Students may use the newspaper column paste-up on the previous page instead of plain writing paper.

What Else Can We

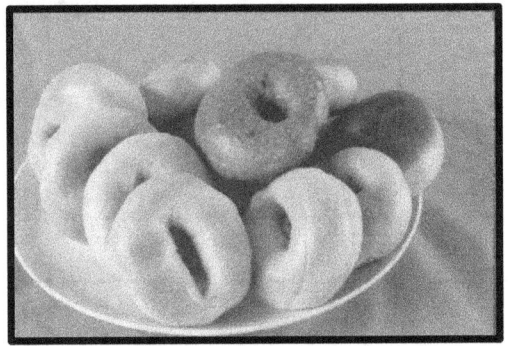

✳ Place 6 bowls in the front of the room labeled **who, what, when, where, why, & how.**
✳ On slips of paper, students will place an appropriate W word in each of the bowls. Shuffle the words in each bowl.
✳ Students will select one slip of paper from each bowl and use those W words to create a newspaper article about the bowl of bagels above.
✳ Students will then share their stories with each other. Most will be humorous and fictitious.

✳ For extra credit, some students may then wish to research the making of bagels and write a true account of *bagels* using authentic photos.

24
Fours

It takes two wings to fly.
Eric Schaub

☞ *Students will team in a Talk, Construct, Shoot and Write experience.*

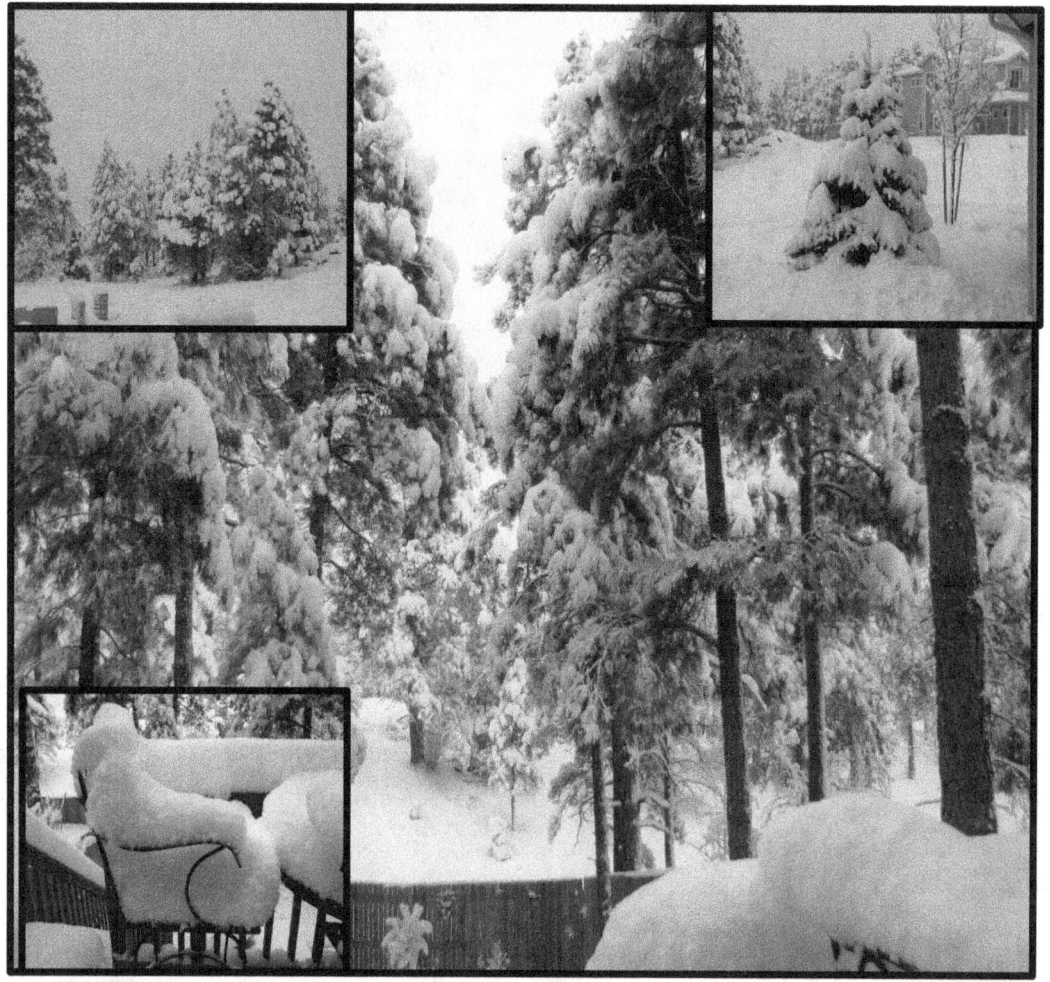

Winter in Northern Arizona

Weather makes for good **brainstorming**, good **construction,** good **shooting,** and good **writing** of stories with an emphasis on *group cooperation*.

Here We Go!

❏ Divide the class into 4 groups. Group ONE will brainstorm ideas that may be conducive to photography and writing. Lead an example with the weather photos on the previous page.

❏ Group TWO will take the consensus idea(s) from Group One and reconstruct the idea (s) into a three dimensional scene or set of sequential photos (as seen in the photos on the previous page)

❏ Group THREE will look at the scene or set, decide on design, balance, composition and harmony of that scene or set, in other words 'fix it' if it needs to be fixed, and 'shoot' the scene.

❏ Group FOUR will use the photograph of the scene and create a writing experience from the photo.

❏ All students will reflect upon the end product and the process and evidence of cooperation of each group's work.

What Else Can We Do

✳ Now with the entire class, do a flip-flop. Group ONE students will write a story about, say the weather.

✳ Group TWO will take the story and create a scene that fits the story, using props, etc.

✳ Group THREE will take a photo of the set that fits the story, then add ONE thing to the photo that wasn't mentioned in the story, or seen in the set (see suggestions below).

✳ All students will listen to the original story, then write chapter two of that story using what they see in the photo that was added.

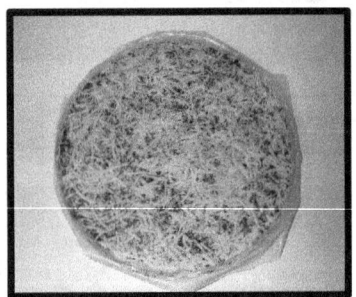 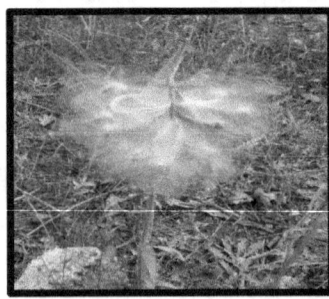 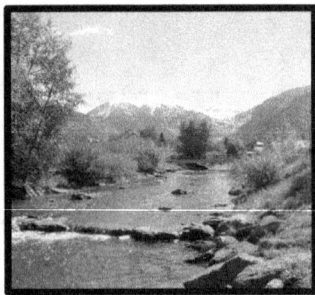

25

Hands and Feet

Let joy keep you. Reach out your hands and take it when it runs by.
Carl Sandburg

☞ *Students will take photos of various 'hands' and reflect upon their uses.*

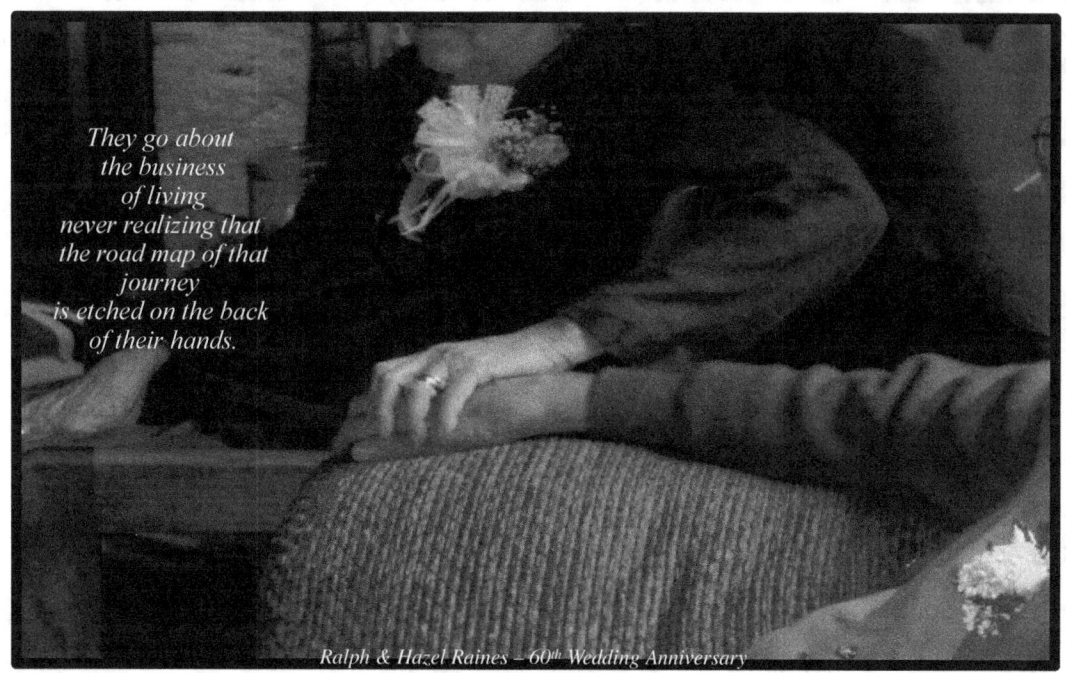

*They go about
the business
of living
never realizing that
the road map of that
journey
is etched on the back
of their hands.*

Ralph & Hazel Raines – 60ᵗʰ Wedding Anniversary

I suppose…	Whenever I…	I wonder…	Time…
The first step…	Open your eyes to…	How strange to…	Now and again…
On one hand….	I often…	The closer I get…	If I look long enough..
Differences occur when..	I reach out to…	Is it possible to…	Fear is less than…

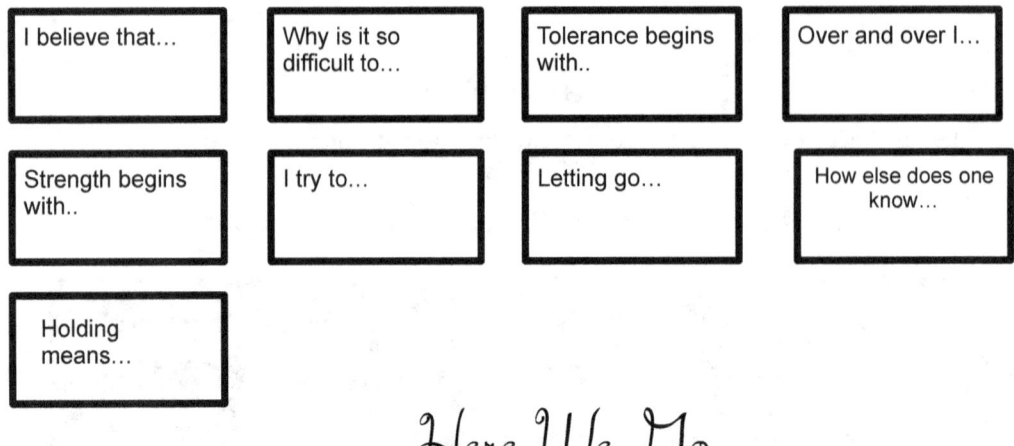

I believe that...	Why is it so difficult to...	Tolerance begins with..	Over and over I...
Strength begins with..	I try to...	Letting go...	How else does one know...
Holding means...			

Here We Go

❑ Look at various 'hands' shown in a current newspaper. Discuss the significance of those hands to the overall events that are occurring in the different photos.

❑ Take photos of hands doing something in the classroom, throughout the school building, or outside.

❑ Write a one sentence or one paragraph explanation that captures the 'essence' of the hand photo.

❑ Use fast drying adhesive bandaging material to create hand masks.

❑ Using the reflective cards on the preceding page to generate conversations

What Else Can We Do

✳ When we talk about hands, we certainly can't forget the power of the camera when it comes to feet.

✳ Look at the different 'feet' on the next page. Take photos of similar feet, or feet found in the woods, on trails, in backyards, or on the playground.

✳ What do they tell you? Where are they going? Where have they been? What is their story? Who do they belong to? How can they be made more interesting? Add to this photo list and create a photo booklet about 'feet'. Let someone else put text into it.

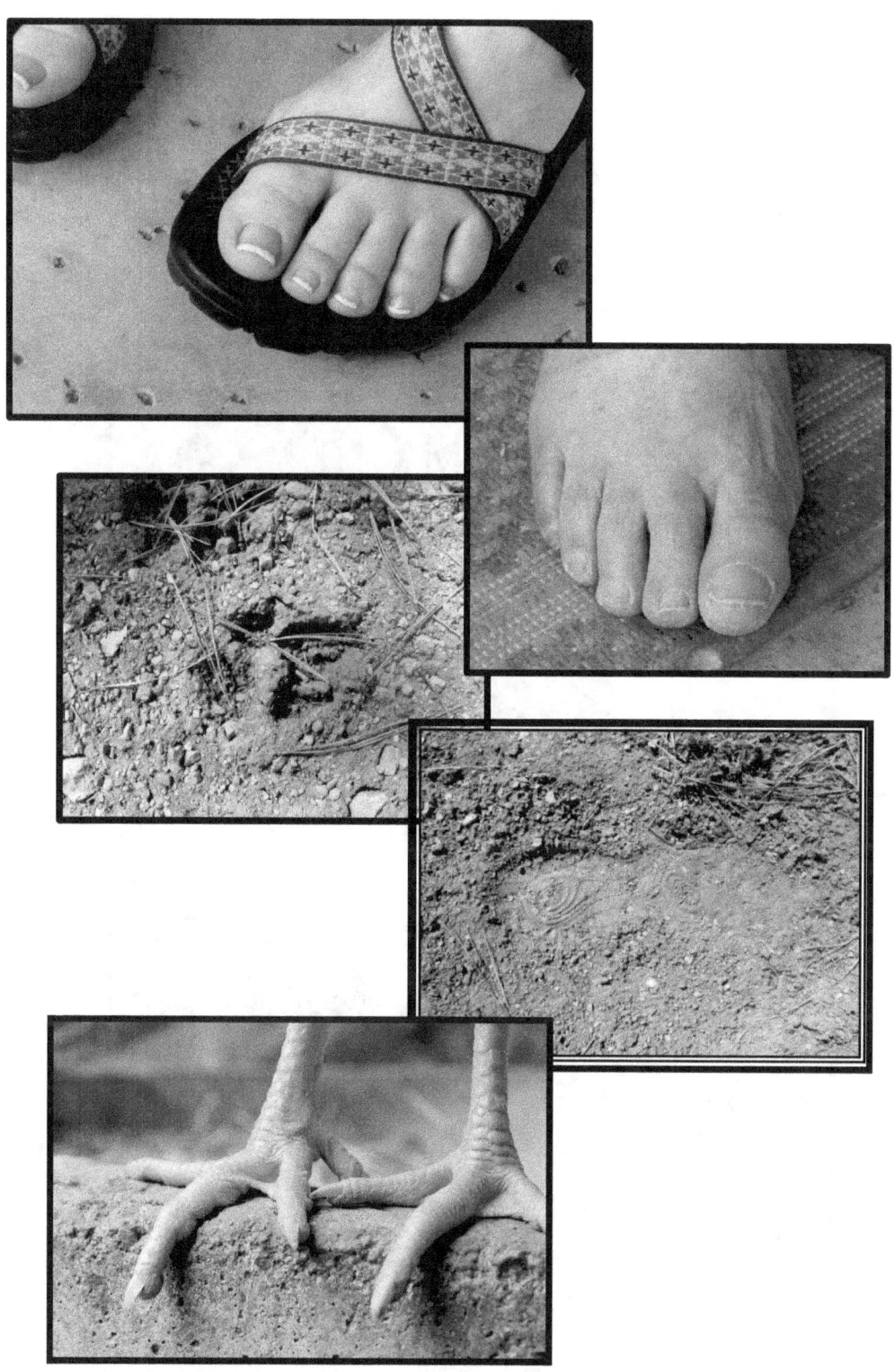

26

I AM

It's never to late to be what you might have
been.
George Elliot

☞ *Students will create I Am photo montages with descriptive words, and build a sculpture of found objects that represent who 'they are'*

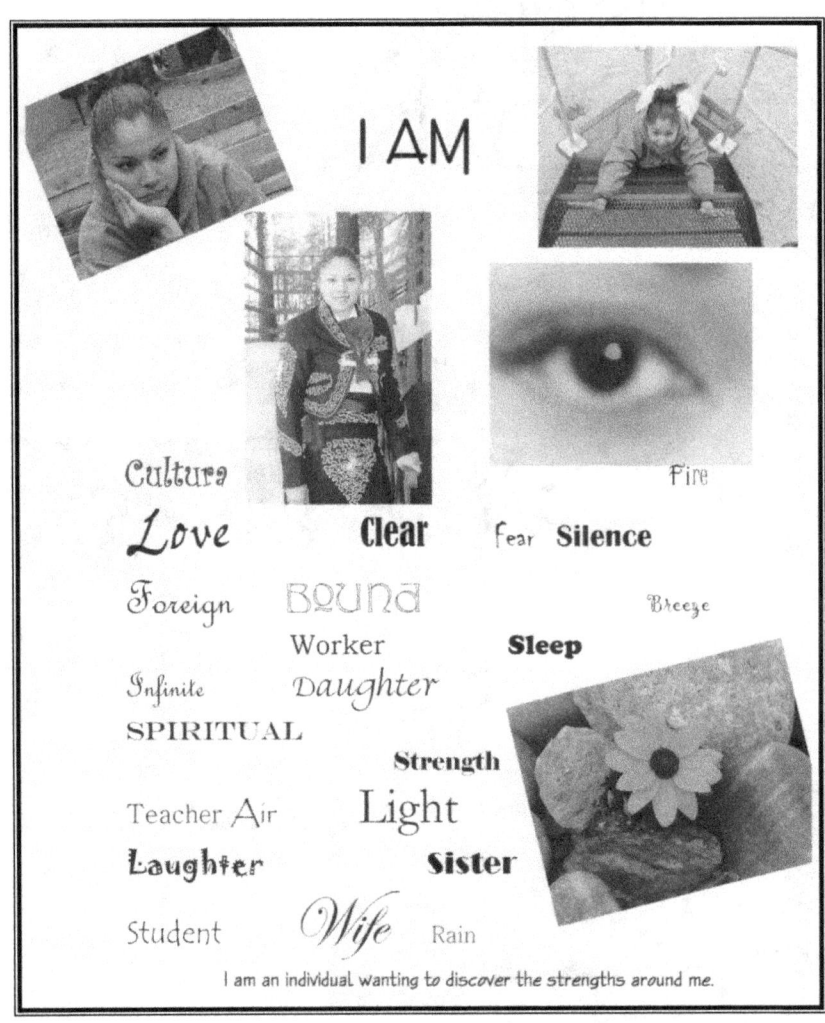

Here We Go

❏ 'Read' the previous montage and draw specific conclusions about the person in the photos.

❏ Figure out what the person might be thinking and write a 3rd person paragraph about it.

❏ Place all the descriptive words in alphabetical order and use as many of those words as possible in writing a fiction story about this person.

❏ Simply tell a story about the person, using all the clues you see on the montage.

❏ Write or tell a story about the cultural heritage of the person in the montage.

❏ Use an I AM photo that has been created by you or a classmate and bring nature into the story.

❏ Create an I AM page about your pet.

❏ Create a 'family' I AM montage and a 'family' I AM sculpture.

❏ Review the 6 Traits of Writing and discuss the value of the I AM montage to the understanding of these traits.

❏ List all the words on your own I AM montage and break them into syllables.

❏ Design a Coat of Arms from an I AM montage, yours or someone else's. Explain symbols and objects.

What Else Can We Do

✳ I AM sculptures are an exciting way to complete the I AM montage photo experience.

✳ Students will use their personal I AM montage and the information from it, create and name a sculpture that is built of found objects to describe the montage in a visual/ bodily kinesthetic way, then display it.

✳Other classmates or classes may ask questions regarding meaning, directions of creating, materials used, thought processes and reflection.

27
I Would Like to Be...

Dogs have owners, cats have staff.
Anonymous

☛ *Students will take animal photos and write a descriptive piece with
'I Would Like to" sentence starters.*

I WOULD LIKE TO

I would like to be a kitty cat with honeyed fur

and polished nails.

I would like to have a tail that functions apart from me and

navigates itself across the panorama of my daily

sights and sounds.

I would like to stretch the length of my body along

the highest ledge above my bookcases

and wait for the sun

to inch its way into the periphery of my space.

I would like to swim in that pool of light

and create the most heavenly of purrs

as I soak in the beam

that comes from just outside the window.

I would like to rearrange flowers with my tongue and

play tennis with the beaded chain that forces the room

to change from night into day.

I would like to dwell near a lake of milk and loiter

behind a door until the right shadow coaxes me to

make a stand.

I would like to arch at my own reflection and

tease the tip of my own ears.

I would like to wash without soap and dry on the

back of the couch.

I would like to stand, for hours, staring at a small home

tucked safely behind a bag of flour in the pantry.

I would like to be a kitty cat with

honeyed fur and polished nails...with honeyed fur and polished nails...

with honeyed fur and polished nails.

Here We Go

❏ List all the words on your own I AM montage and break them into syllables.

❏ Students will take photos of random animals, pets, or favorite animals.

❏ They will write original stories or poems explaining 'how' they would 'feel' as the animal and 'what' they would 'do' as that animal.

❏ Teacher will use these stories as imagery experiences and let classmates find various endings to the stories.

❏ Class will discuss the new images that come from listening to each other's stories. New or interesting words or phrases will be listed on the board and discussed.

❏ Students will select favorite phrases or sentences that 'capture' the animal character of someone else's writing piece and discuss the impact or power of that phrase or sentence on the overall success of the piece of writing.

What Else Can We Do

✱ This exercise focuses on an extemporaneous 'telling' of a story about an animal.

✱ Students will use this photo or take an original photo of an animal and use the animal as a central character to a story with a different theme. The various themes include..

Mystery

Social Issue

Good Luck Story

Adventure

Humorous

Dilemma

Heroism

Other

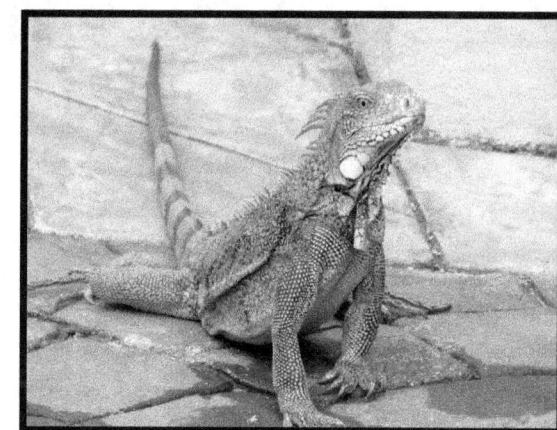

28
Imagined Moments

To imagine is everything. To know is nothing at all.
Anatole Francois

☞ *Students will draw something unrelated on an existing photo and write about   or discuss the completed photo.*

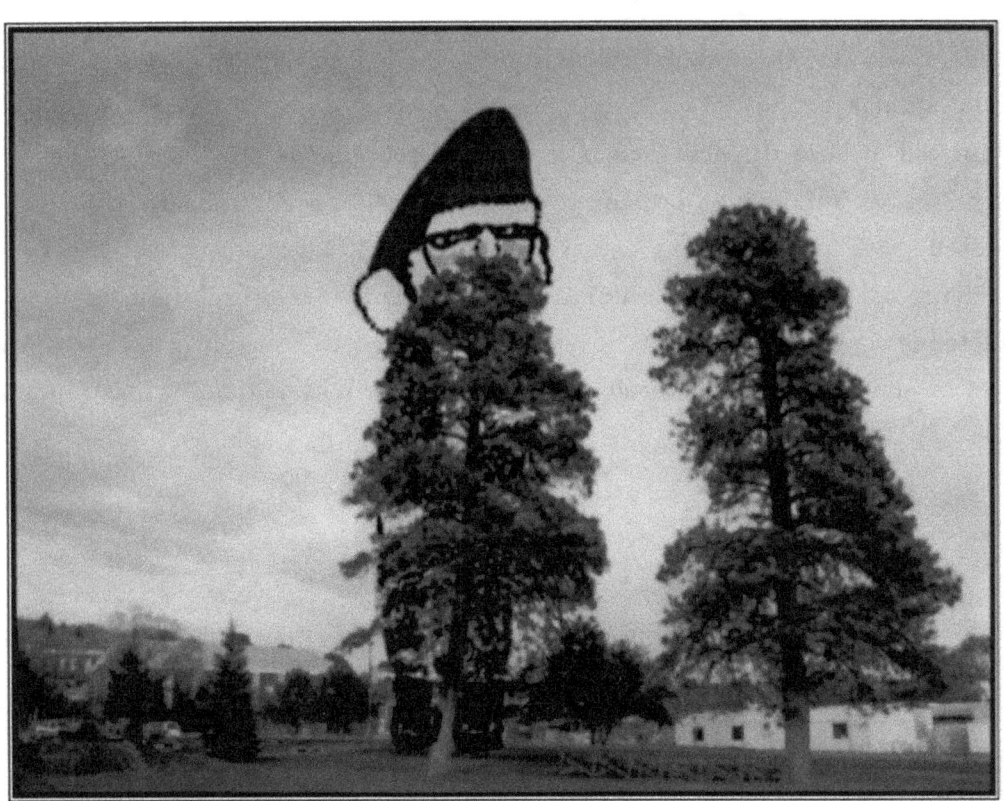

Here We Go

❏ Look at the giant Santa hiding behind the tree on the previous page. Brainstorm all the story ideas that can come from that. In threes, students will write a beginning, middle, and end to this photo.

❏ These *imagined moments* may be the most fun ideas in the book. Students will use candid shots as the ones below and draw *themselves or something else* in the photo. They will then write or tell a story that comes from the photo.

❏ Teacher may also read the *imagery story* accompanying this old, often used photo below, and have students create an ending.

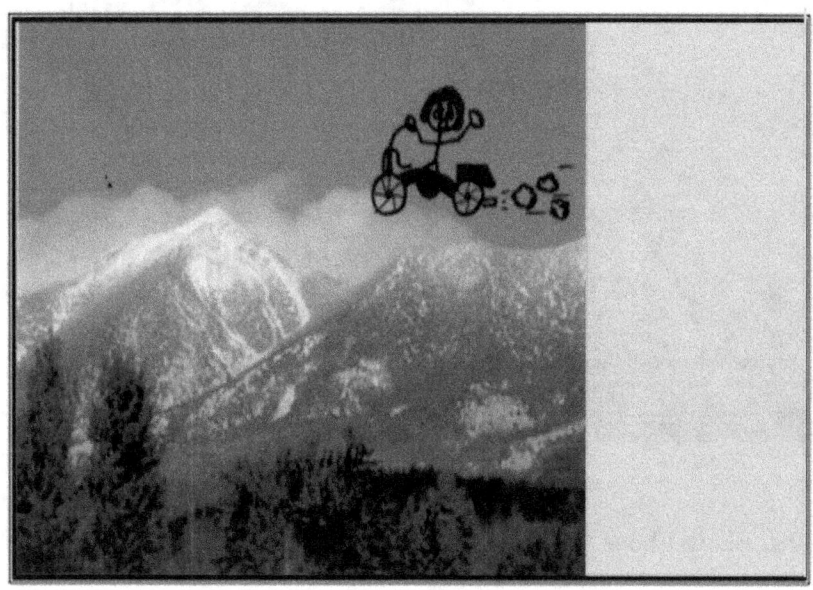

CLOSE YOUR EYES as I read this imagined moment.

"You wake up and realize that you are late for school. You jump on your bike and make a mad dash trying to get there in time. You know you won't make it so you say a magic word and your bike flies through the sky, past the local mountain and toward your school. Suddenly you see that you aren't going to make it. You land in a _____. How do you get to school on time?"

What Else Can We Do

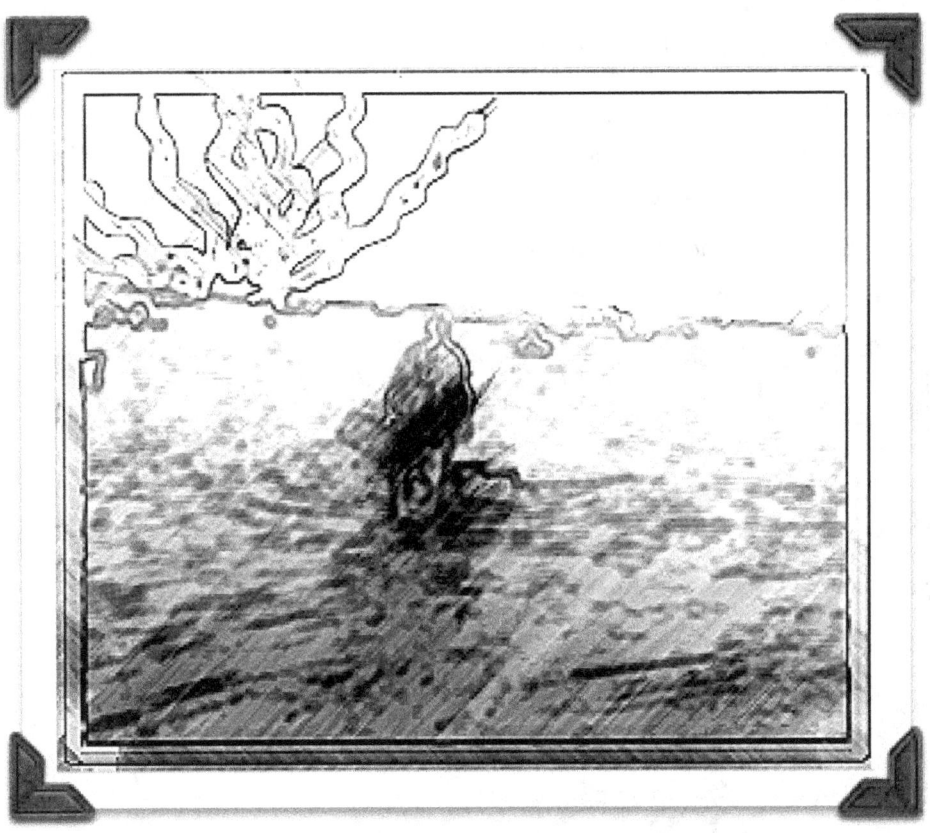

✱   Use this tweaked photo above to create an *imagined moment* story with one of these themes.

Bizarre	Leading to Another Story	Impossible
Movie-Like	Futuristic	Likely
Inevitable	Normal	Scary
Unlikely	Catastrophic	Mundane
Normal	Three-Part-Story b	

29
Middle

Stories don't have a middle or an end anymore.
They usually have a beginning that never stops beginning
Steven Spielberg

☛ *Students will use an original photo to create the 'middle' of a story.*

The Blue Heron

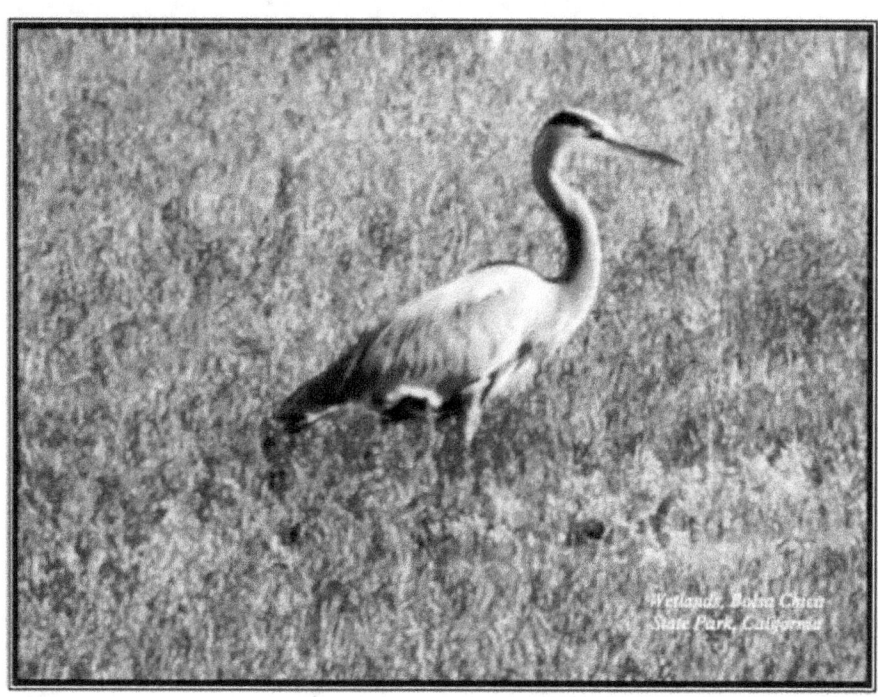

(Beginning)...From afar, the grassy surface looked like waves of multicolored water, dense with algae, light with foam, darkened by the undercurrent of unseen swells and speckled gently with bits and pieces of paper and sand. Upon closer examination, however, as the grass became grass, and sky became sky, something appeared...a statue unfolding into arc and curve and roundness and stately stance...a blue heron. With feathers pointed and colorful hues dripping upon and immersing into themselves, the blue heron took residence in the marsh.

The heron stood with the grace of time and observed that which could be seen and not seen. Its eyes penetrated the slightest shadow, the quietest sound, the smallest movement...a perfect given moment. It stood leaf still until it could stand still no longer

What goes in the middle?

(Ending)...When the chaos ended, the blue heron leveled its wingspan and bulleted its way toward another section of the marsh. Its gentle landing gear touched the soft, loamy soil that became the perfect place for stopping.

And then it stopped, the blue heron. It stopped and looked around. It stopped and calmed its small bird heart, and let the day ease it into safety, not listening, for now, to the clock of that heartbeat.

Here We Go

❏ The middle of a piece of writing is often the hardest part of the writing process. We can begin things, and end them with some writing flair, most of the time, but the middle is a bit of a bugaboo. This activity may help.

❏ Find pieces of well known, short narratives, cut out the middle of each narrative.

❏ Students will take a photo representing the piece of writing, and write an original 'middle' to accompany the rest of the narrative and

❏ Students may use the heron photo and story on the precious page to bet them started, or teacher may write a beginning and end to that photo and let the students create the middle.

What Else Can We Do

✳ Use familiar objects that can be found in the classroom or around the school.

✳ Students will write a *middle piece* for one photo and use the other two as the beginning and the end of the piece.

✳ Or, let students decide how to use the 3 photos together or separately in a writing experience focusing on *middle*.30

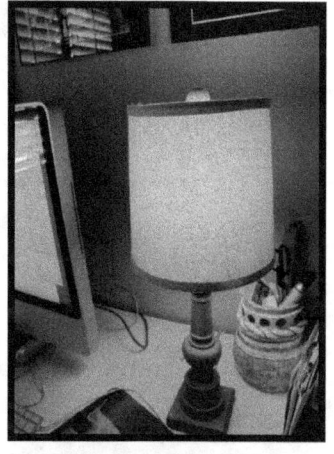

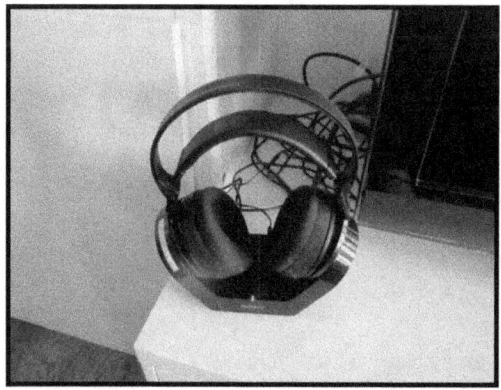

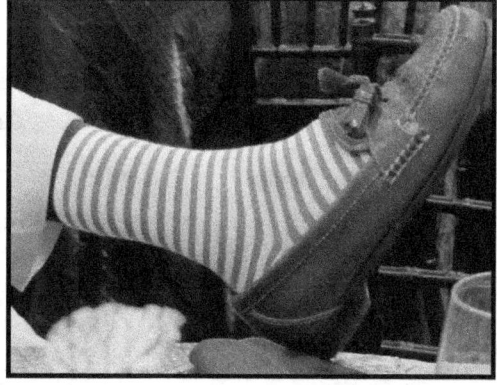

30
This Miata is So Red That...

Exaggeration is a truth that has lost its temper. Khalil Gibran

☛ *Create written exaggeration with photos to complete the phrase... This ___ is so ___ that ___.*

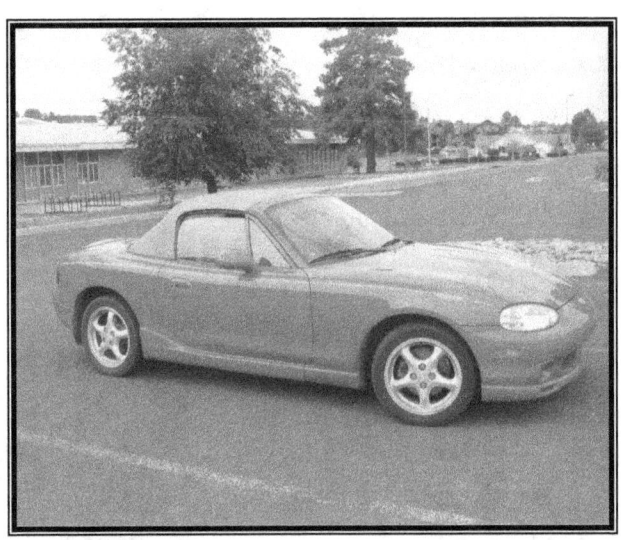

RED IS....

Mazda	fire	lava	anger	apple	joy	speed
holiday	circus	tomato	heart	energy	Mars	cherry
storm	beets	heat	chaos	robin	blood	tulip
sunset	temper	pepper	danger	Coke	rash	sunstroke
zeal	alarm	rhubarb	Target	fever	stop sign	balloon
Christmas		flag	happy	warning	boiling	China
harm	algae	clown	excitement	allergy	lollipop	firetruck
paprika	carpet	earache	scar	pencil	type-A	rose
race car	cranberry	valentine	Lucy	strawberry	aggression	
firetruck	ladybug	thermometer				

Here We Go

❏ Bring several objects or photos of objects to class with different shapes, sizes, colors, weights, and textures.

❏ Students will use these objects as guides to complete this phrase,

This_____is so_____that___. Example: This <u>Miata</u> is so <u>red</u> that ____.
Geraniums get jealous.
I need a thermometer when I drive.
People get a sunburn when I pass them.
Tomatoes blush.
Watermelons roll over and play dead.
Firetrucks shudder.
Mars wears a shawl.
Roses wilt on the bush.
Target closes its doors.

❏ Students will now choose words such as *small, big, flat, fuzzy, green, yellow, bright, long, short, cold, tall, shaky,* and so on as descriptors to guide them to the kind of photo they will take in order to complete the created sentence.

❏ Students will take the shot and then create 5 to 7 varied responses to the above phrase. Share the responses in class.

❏ Students will use their own physical clues to complete the phrase. Example: *Tim is so fast that a jackrabbit can't catch him.*

What Else Can We Do

✱ Here's a little art project that works well with this exercise. A student will draw something like a <u>tall tree</u> on the board.

✱ Other students will draw something onto this tree drawing that complete this phrase, *This tree is so___, that _____.*

✱ Emphasize creativity, humor and intelligence.

This tree is so tall that birds fall to the ground from lack of oxygen.

31
Point of View

I have wanted you to see out of my eyes so many times.
Elizabeth Berg

☛ *Students will 'give speech' to inanimate objects.*

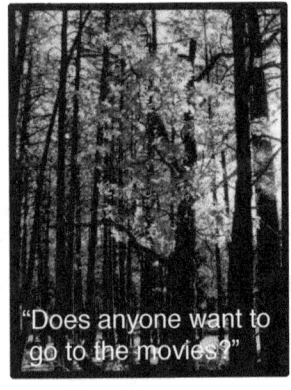
"Does anyone want to go to the movies?"

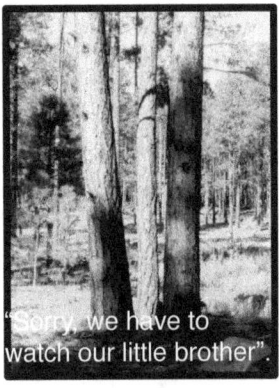
"Sorry, we have to watch our little brother".

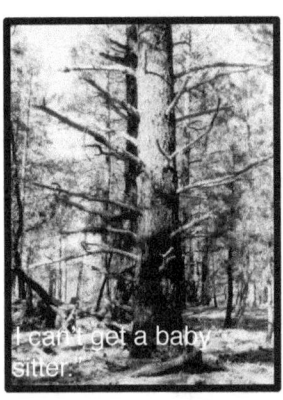
"I can't get a baby sitter."

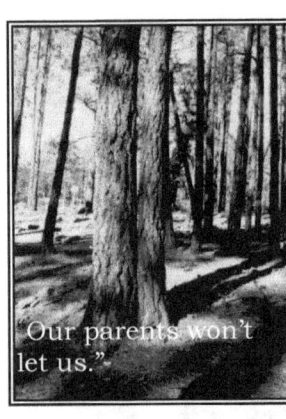
"Our parents won't let us."

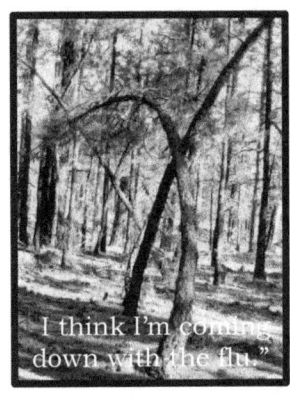
I think I'm coming down with the flu."

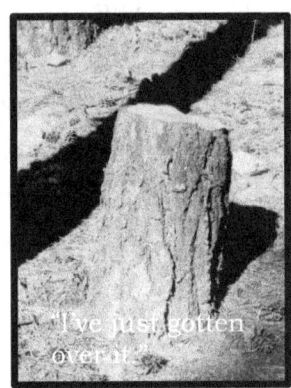
"I've just gotten over it."

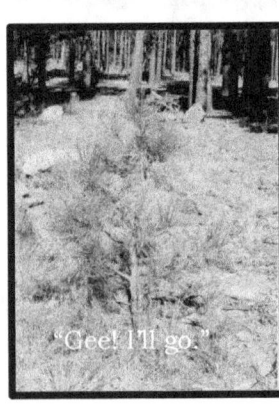
"Gee! I'll go."

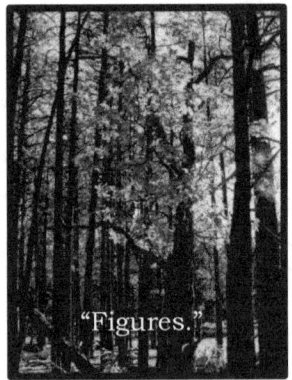
"Figures."

Inanimate Objects: Give inanimate objects the freedom of speech and tell a story using only one sentence per photo. Also retell through 1st person, 3rd person, pantomime, verbal conversation or even puppet skits.

Here We Go

❏ Choose 5 inanimate objects from the room. Take photos of those objects and write a 1st person *point of view* story regarding birth, childhood, adulthood, and death.

❏ Use shadows of humans and write *point of view* stories.

❏ Look at generic photos. Select one part of each photo and discuss what that part might be saying about the rest of the photo.

❏ View two photos and discuss how the photos create various points of view.

❏ Take one random shot and shots of 5 different people. Write *point of views* from the 5 different people about the information in the random shot: Minister, Football Player, Mayor, Amazon Tribesman, Baby, Wealthy Person, School Principal, Parent

❏ Shoot various doors. Convey *point of views* regarding what is 'behind' each door.

What Else Can We Do

✳ Masks are interesting mediums to use when offering students various ways of writing through points of view. If time allows, have students create their own masks out of anything, and write or 'become' the mask personas. If not, use public domain mask photos such as these below.

✳ Here are some suggested point of view lead ins: aliens, next door neighbor, new kid in school, circus performer, new Halloween costume, long lost relative who has come to visit for the first time.

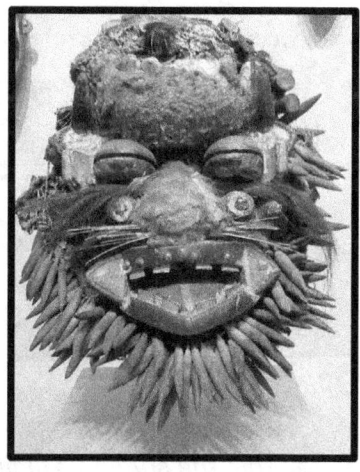

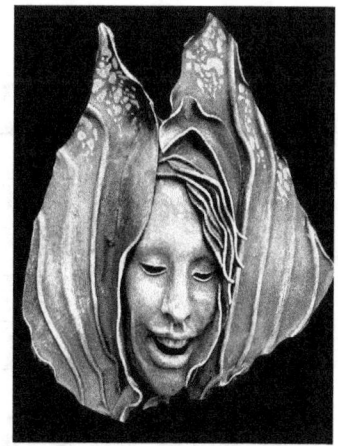

32
Prepositional Phrases
Ending a phrase with a preposition is something up with which I will not put.
Winston Churchill

☛ *Students will use photos to enhance knowledge of prepositional phrases.*

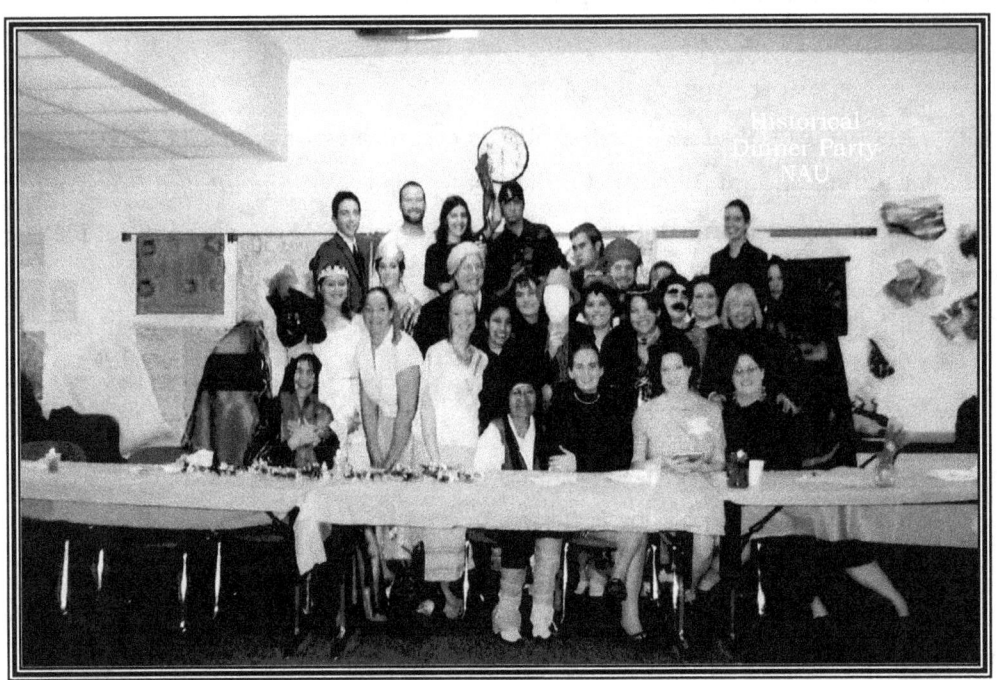

A preposition is a word that connects a noun or pronoun to the rest of the sentence.

1.The students were_____.

a. *during the photo shoot*

2.The clock was _____.

b. *according to the professor*

3.The students' feet were _____.

c .*beside Eleanor of Aquitaine*

4.Geronimo _____.

d. *at the table*

5.The bulletin board was _____.

e. *among the young men and women*

6.Sir Francis Drake stood _____.

f. *on the wall*

7.The class smiled _____.

g. *behind the group*

8. Beethoven scrunched _____.

h. *below the desks*

9.The project seemed _____.

i. *in the front*

10._____, this was fun.

j. *within the student's limits of endurance*

Here We Go

AT	BY	IN
ON	NEAR	TO
FROM	DOWN	OFF
THROUGH	OUT	PAST
UP	OF	FOR
WITH	LIKE	

One Syllable Prepositions

ABOUT	ALONG	BELONG	DURING
ABOVE	AMONG	BENEATH	EXCEPT
ACROSS	AROUND	BESIDE	INSIDE
AFTER	BEFORE	BETWEEN	OUTSIDE
AGAINST	BEHIND	BEYOND	OVER
UNDER			

Two-Syllable Prepositions

INTO	UPON	WITHOUT
ONTO	WITHIN	
	THROUGHOUT	

Compound Prepositions

ACCORDING TO	OUT OF	ON ACCOUNT OF	ASIDE FROM
PRIOR TO	OWING TO	INSIDE OF	BY MEANS OF
IN FRONT OF	SUBSEQUENT TO	BECAUSE OF	AS TO

Multi-Word Prepositions

❏ Put this list of prepositions in the room so students have a chance to see them at all times.

❏ Teacher will call out an object in the room. Students will create a prepositional phrase connected to that object

What Else Can We Do

✳   Simply find a unique photo and give students freedom to use as many prepositions or prepositional phrases as they can.

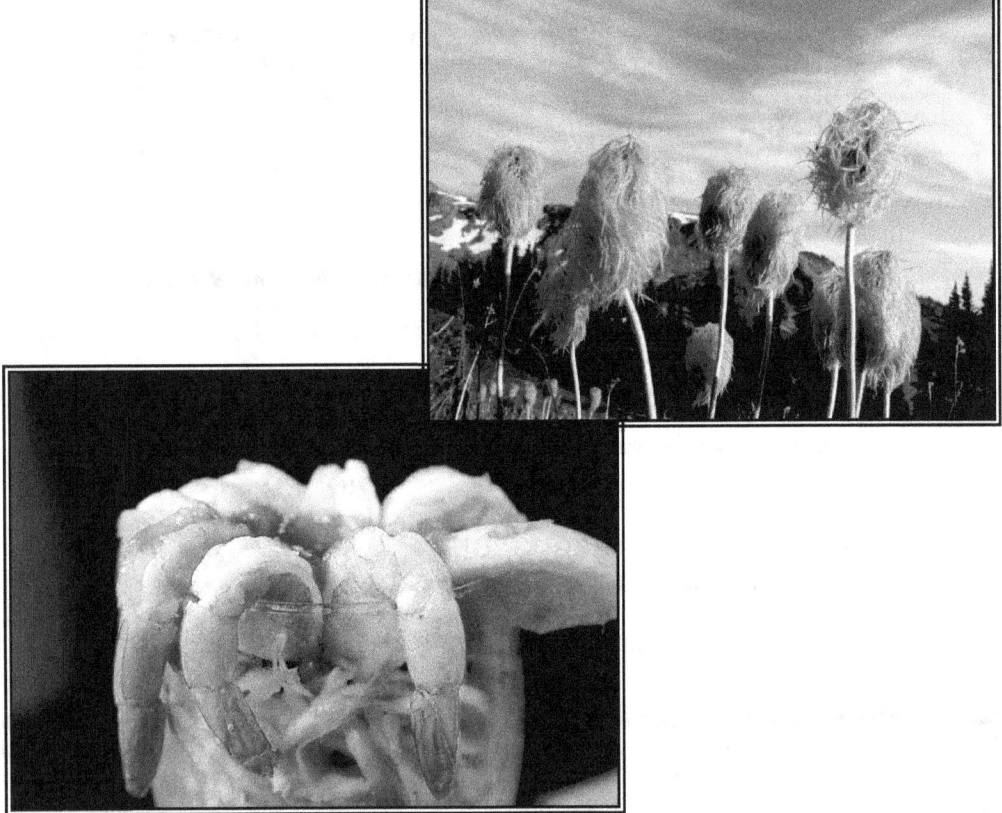

33
Prior Knowledge
Without experiencing a thing one cannot gain knowledge from it.
Anonymous

☛ *Students will use photos to bring about prior knowledge of certain similar experiences.*

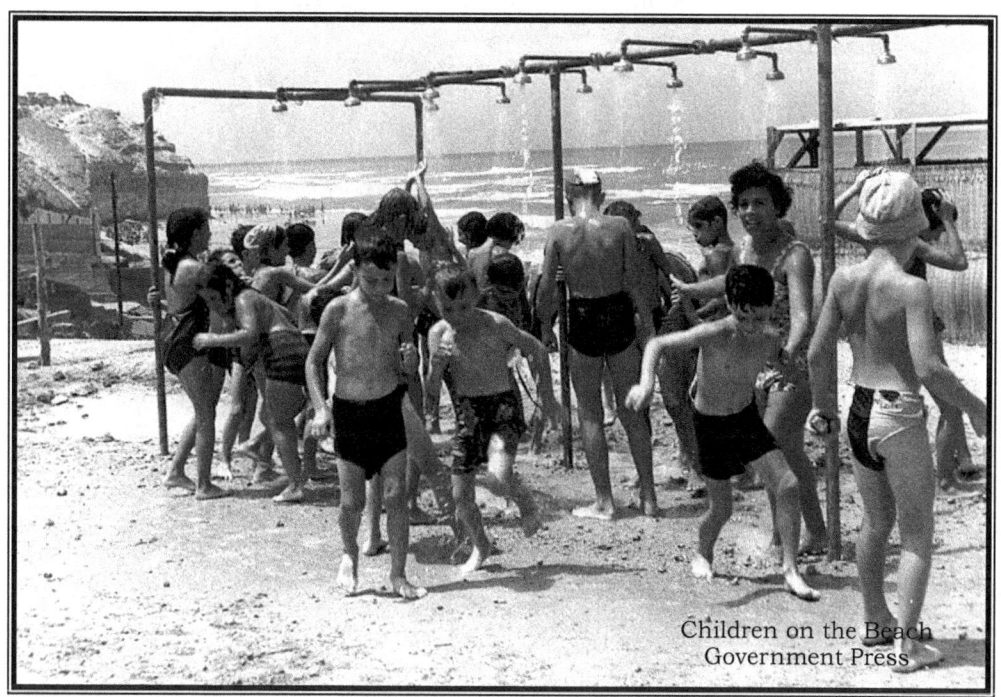

Children on the Beach
Government Press

As you sit here looking at this photo, think of all the times you have been to the beach. Think of the sand and the water and the footprints. Remember the wind and the sound of the waves and the feel of the waves themselves. Think about all the different people you passed on the beach; the children with pails, the elderly couple holding onto each other, the group of boys running and shoving each other toward the water.

As you sit here looking at this photo, think of all the time times you have been to the beach. Think of the sand in your shoes, the squishy sound as you walk, the nagging thought of how long it will take to dry out these shoes.

As you sit here looking at this photo, tell yourself everything you know about the beach and your last trip there. As you sit here looking at this photo, think of all the times you have been to the beach. Think of the sand and the water and the footprints. Remember the wind and the sound of the waves and the feel of the waves themselves. Think about all the different people you passed on the beach; the children with pails,

75

the elderly couple holding onto each other, the group of boys running and shoving each other toward the water.

As you sit here looking at this photo, think of all the time times you have been to the beach. Think of the sand in your shoes, the squishy sound as you walk, the nagging thought of how long it will take to dry out these shoes.

As you sit here looking at this photo, tell yourself everything you know about the beach and your last trip there.

Here We Go

The process of constructing meaning through reading, writing, speaking, and listening is based on the prior knowledge that individuals bring to the situation.
(Adams and Bertram, 1980)

❏ Look at a random photo and discuss general things you see in the photo. In other words, 'read' the photo.

❏ Now discuss personal experiences or memories that come to mind upon observing the photo.

❏ Select one of those personal experiences or memories and write about that experience or memory.

❏ Share those written experiences with each other, asking appropriate questions as you go along.

❏ Teacher will ask students reflective questions such as:

- What is the favorite part of the written memory?
- What part of the photo triggered that memory?

What Else Can We Do

✱ Have children tell you everything they know about either Halloween or Thanksgiving as it applies to their personal lives.

✱ Students will then shoot or bring to school a memory photo of their favorite holiday.

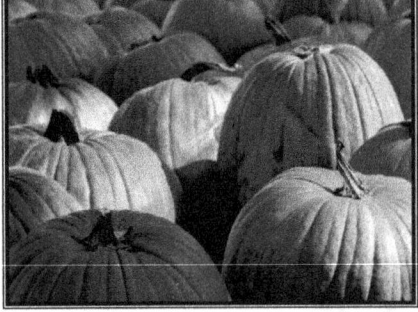

34

"Reading" a Photograph

A good photograph is knowing where to stand.
Ansel Adams

☛ *Students will use photos to enhance their ability to see details.*

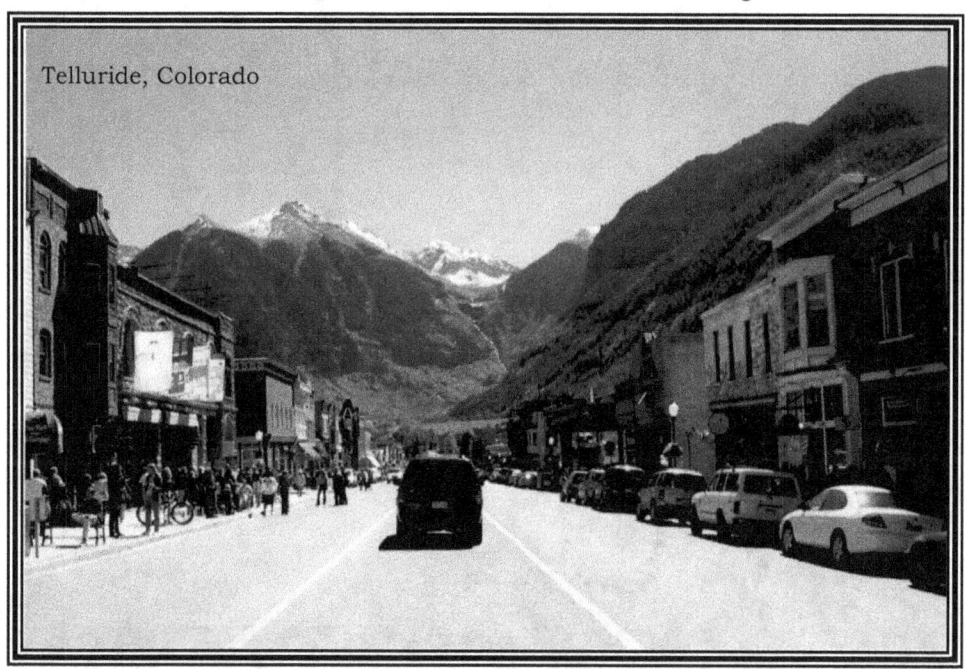

Telluride, Colorado

To 'read' a photograph look at all parts of the photo then ask questions such as these.

Where is the camera?	Tell everything you see in the photo.	When and where was this photo taken?	What is the photographer's intention?
What is the photographer trying to communicate?	A similar moment happened when..	Describe the using 10 adjectives	This photo reminds me of..
Tell me 5 true facts about this photo.	5 misconceptions about this photo	What part of the photo draws you	How would you reshoot this photo
Where would you put yourself in this photo	If this photo were a CD, what would the title be?	If the camera were facing you in this photo, what would it be shooting, ie, What is behind you?	

Here We Go

❏ Take a family photo and ask these 'reading' questions about the photo.

- What is the 'mood' of the photo?
- What does the family photo 'say'?
- Describe the expressions on each person's face.
- Describe the relationships to each other.

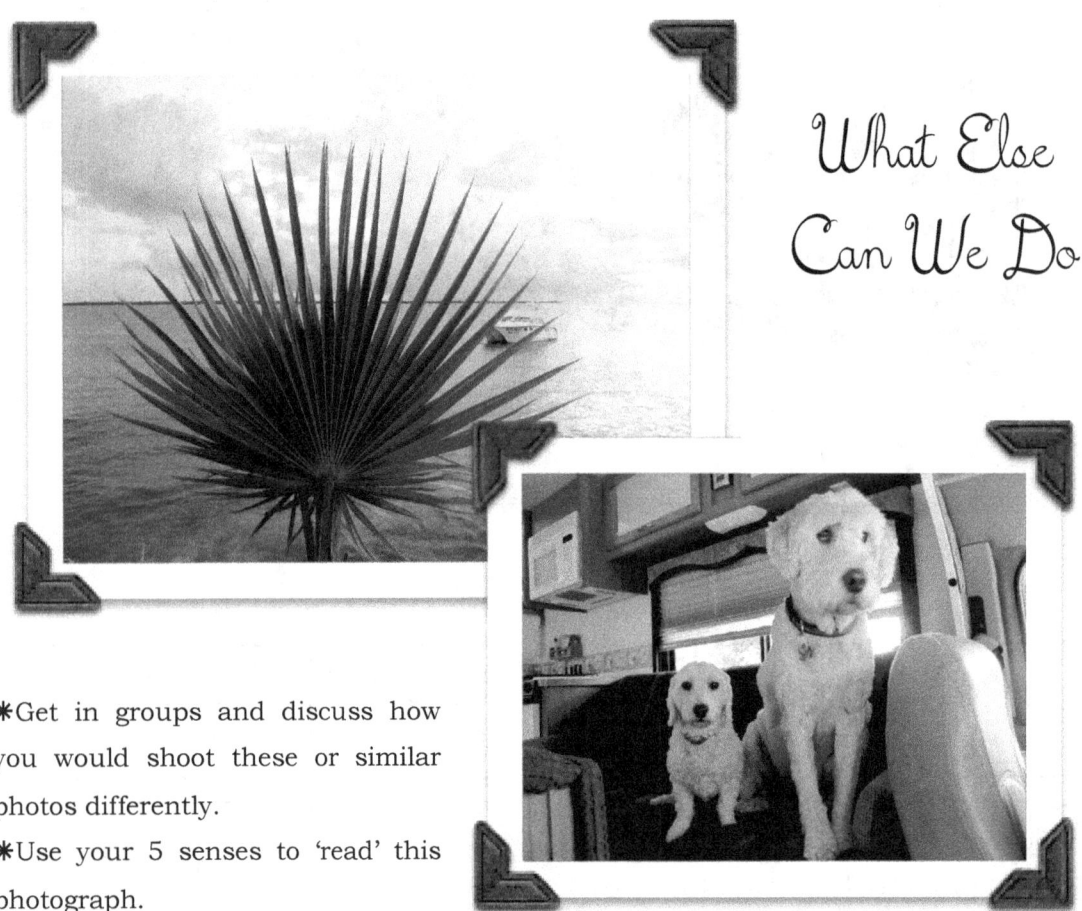

What Else Can We Do

✴Get in groups and discuss how you would shoot these or similar photos differently.

✴Use your 5 senses to 'read' this photograph.

✴"Read' this in mathematical terms.

✴Draw conclusions after 'reading' this photo.

✴Teacher tells the story of this photo.

✴Write a journal entry about this photo.

35
Self Portrait

Often we can't tell for sure if a photo is a self-portrait unless
the photographer tells us so.
John Suler

☛ *Students will take a self-portrait in a personalized scene.*

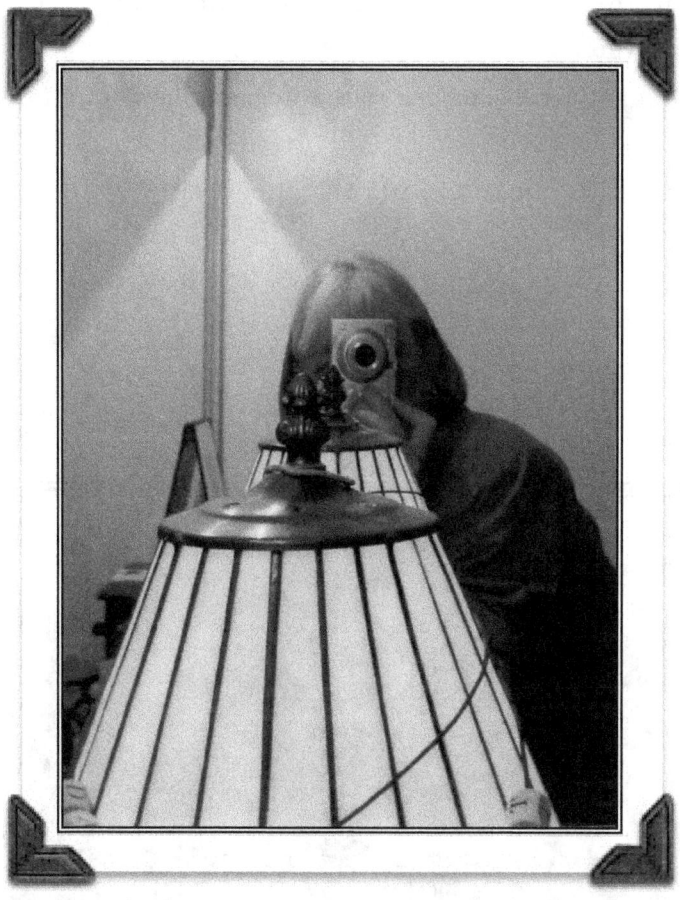

A **self-portrait** is a portrait you take of yourself. You are trying to tell everyone 'who you are'. And that can be done in various ways. They can be subjective as well as objective. In a subjective shot we almost certainly know the photo was taken by the subject, as seen above. An objective shot is often done by someone else showing 'how they see that person.

Self-portraits can be planned or spontaneous, and they can also be 'framed'; that is a photo is taken of one aspect of the subject. For example, if the person uses his or hands often, then only the hand is photographed to 'tell the world about that part of himself."

Here We Go

❏ Take a self portrait in a 'created environment' that best describes you.

❏ Take a photo of one aspect of you that you think defines you best.

❏ Take a 'symbolic' self-portrait; that is, create something that shows 'who you are', in a non-human way. In other words use light, shadows, nature, art, architecture, clay, objects, to show who you are.

❏ Take a self-portrait and have someone else write your 'life's story." Now write your own.

❏ Take a self-portrait and critique all parts of that portrait. What do you like? What would you change?

❏ Find other well-known self-portraits. Read about why they chose to paint or photograph themselves.

What Else Can We Do

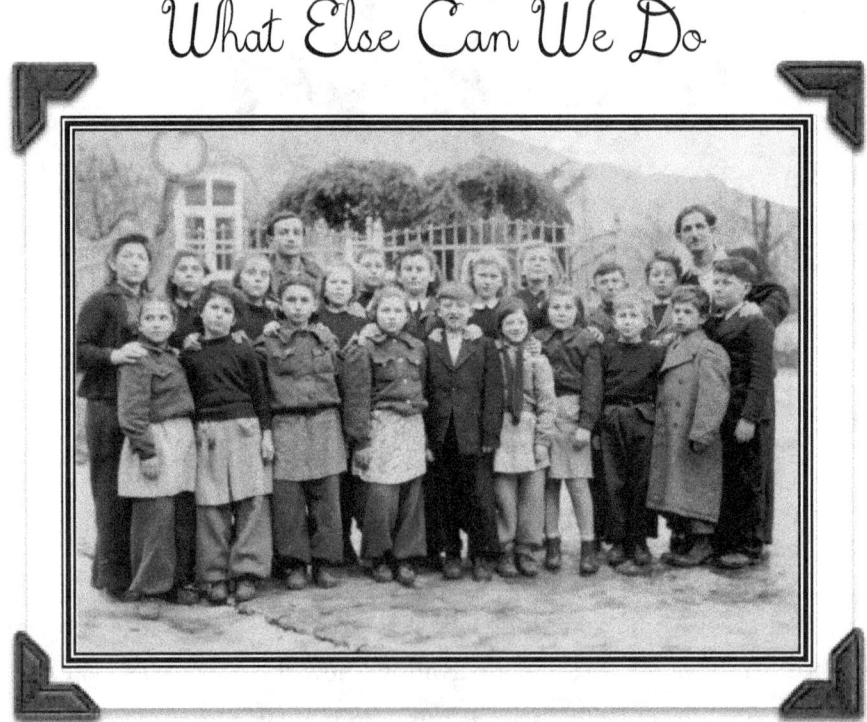

Displaced children, 1946,

✳ Take a spontaneous class photo. Ask the kids to find a place in the room, close together and take the shot. Then ask each one of them to look at themselves in the group photo and answer these questions.

- Look how I...
- Wow! I...
- Do others see me as...
- I never noticed that I ...
- What a surprise to see me...
- Am I in the center of things?
- Do I look shy?
- Do I 'stand out'?
- Am I hiding?
- Am I "invisible"?
- What have I forgotten about myself
  that this photo reveals?

❋ Select one of the children in the photo on the previous page. Now answer the questions above as a *displaced child after World War 11.*

❋ Select one of the children in the photo on the previous page and write about what his or her life was *before* the war...and then *after.*

❋ Take a photo of yourself and place it in this photo of the children. How are you different from them? Discuss those differences.

❋ How old are those children now and where do you think they are?

❋ Answer these reflective questions as a class..

Where does my 'head' go when I seen this photo?

What would I have done if I were one of those children?

What does 'displaced' mean to you?

Why are their clothes worn so differently?

36

Sequencing
It's your story, run with it.
Tom Egan

☛ *Students will compile dozens of their own pet shots, mix them up, and create a sequencing story from 7-10 of them.*

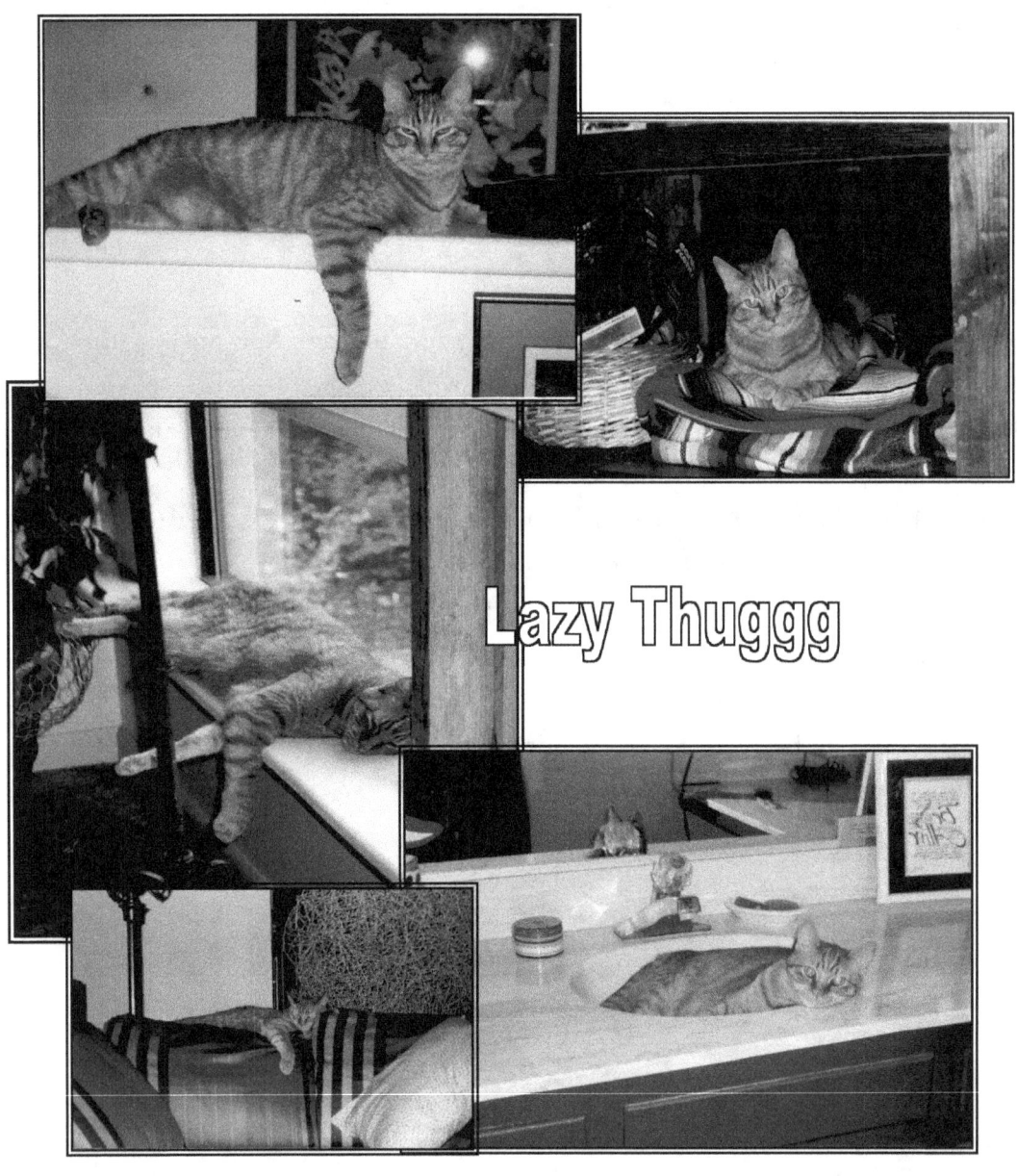

Lazy Thuggg

Here We Go

❏ Ask all the students to take 3-5 photos of one of their pets. Bring the photos back and teacher will mix them all together. Groups of 4 will select 6-7 photos and either write a sequential story or tell it to the rest of the class as they show each photo in the order of their story. Story themes can be:

> mystery
>
> hero/heroine
>
> travel
>
> surprise
>
> something lost
>
> vacation
>
> other

❏ Pairs will take turns placing 5 photos on the desk and the other person tells the story spontaneously using the 5 photos.

❏ Groups will create a storyline and place photos in sequential order. Another group will use the storyline and photos to write a group story. Groups will create a storyline and place photos in sequential order. Another group will use the storyline and photos to write a group story.

What Else Can We Do

✱ Try adding another character with your sequence stories and use only two photos. Looks like Thugg wants desperately to share her TV story with someone, maybe her best friend, Booo.

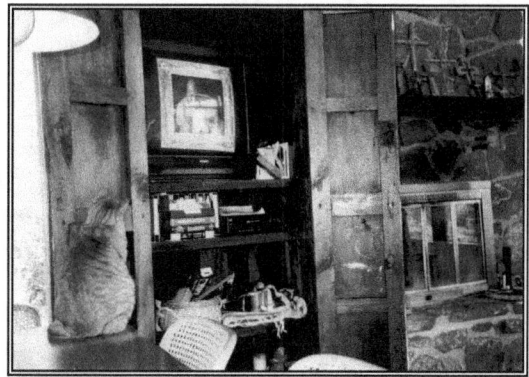 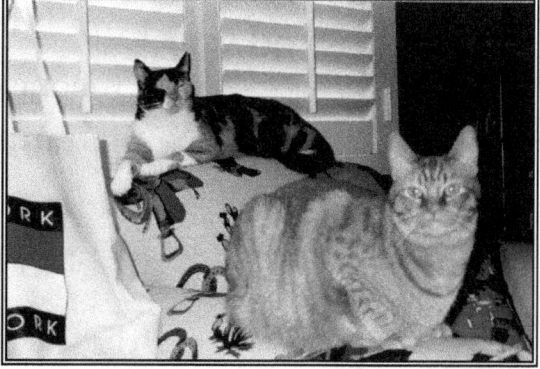

37
Synonyms
A synonym is a word you use when you can't spell the word you first thought of .
Burt Bacharach

☛ *Students will use photos to create a broader list of usable synonyms.*

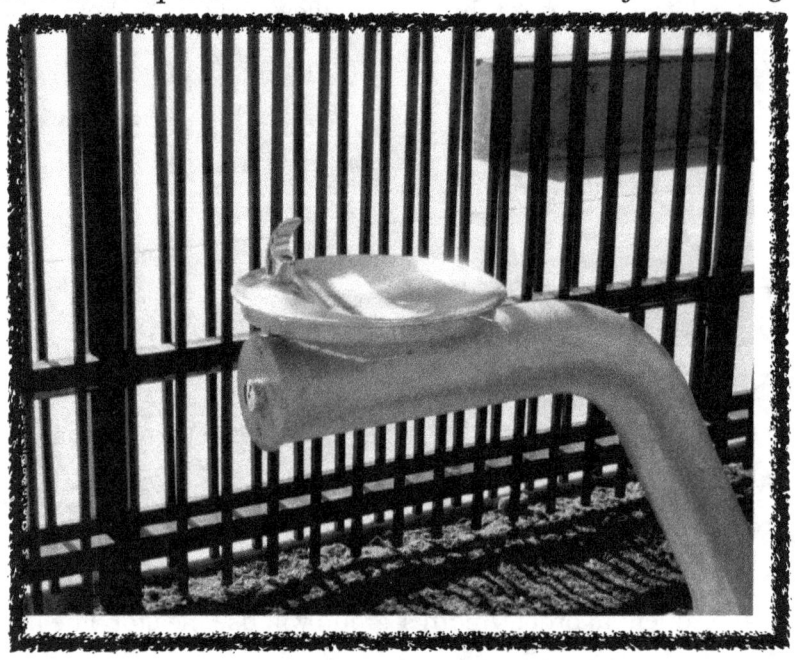

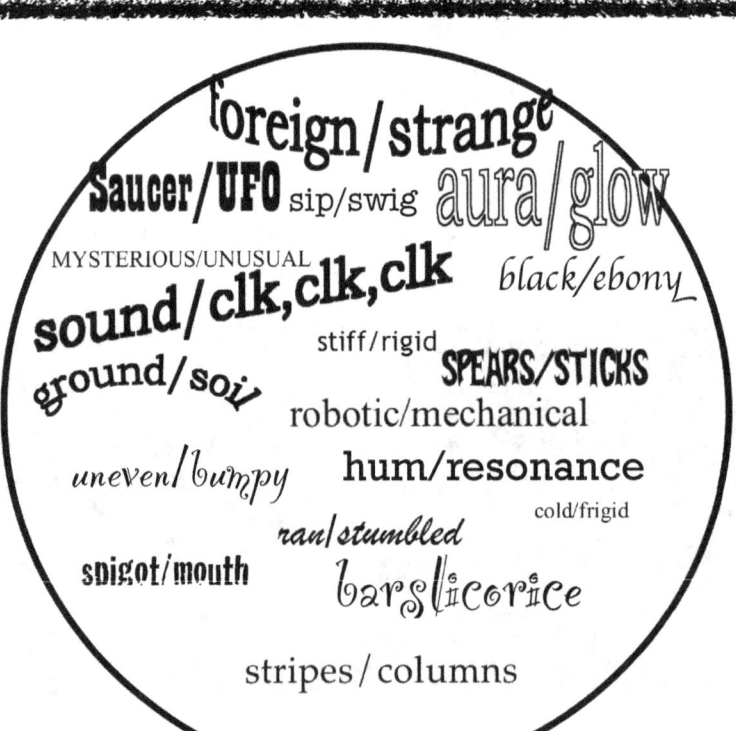

foreign/strange
Saucer/UFO sip/swig aura/glow
MYSTERIOUS/UNUSUAL
sound/clk,clk,clk   black/ebony
                    stiff/rigid
ground/soil   SPEARS/STICKS
              robotic/mechanical
uneven/bumpy   hum/resonance
                              cold/frigid
              ran/stumbled
spigot/mouth   barslicorice

stripes/columns

Here We Go

❑ Look at the two identical stories below. Discuss the choices of synonyms and see which is a more enriched telling because of the different synonyms. Now, retell or rewrite the story using other synonyms that mean almost the same as the underlined or spontaneously using the 5 photos.

❑ Take a photo and break in down into verbs, nouns, and adjectives. Create synonyms spontaneously using the 5 photos.

❑ Write a story about the photo using as many descriptive words as possible that were 'uncovered' by looking at the photo.

(A) *I was walking through a park one day and <u>ran</u> across this interesting sight. The first time I <u>saw</u> it, it looked like so many different things. The <u>stripes</u> of <u>black</u> <u>bars</u> standing stiffly like <u>sticks</u> reminded me of something <u>strange</u> and <u>unusual.</u> Had the wind blown through them, the musical <u>sound</u> would have <u>hummed</u> a <u>mechanical</u> tune.*

At second glance, I noticed a device that sat above the <u>wavy</u> <u>ground.</u> Was this a tiny <u>saucer</u> bathing in a nameless <u>glow</u>? Had it landed and raised its <u>bent</u> <u>spigot</u> to grab anything in its reach. Surely not!

The day was getting to be quite cold so I took a <u>sip</u> of water and went home.

(B) *I was walking through a park one day and <u>stumbled</u> across this interesting sight. The first time I <u>spied</u> it, it looked like so many different things. The <u>columns</u> of <u>ebony</u> <u>licorice</u>, standing stiffly like <u>spears,</u> reminded me of something <u>foreign</u> and <u>mysterious.</u> Had the wind blown through the <u>rigid</u> <u>sticks,</u> the musical <u>clk,clk,clk</u> would have <u>resonated</u> a <u>robotic</u> tune.*

At second glance, I noticed a device that sat above the <u>uneven</u> <u>soil.</u> Was this a tiny <u>UFO</u> bathing in a nameless <u>aura?</u> Had it landed and raised its <u>curved</u> <u>mouth</u> to grab anything in its reach. Surely not!

The day was getting to be quite <u>frigid</u> so I took a <u>swig</u> of water and went home.

> **Now, think of a 3rd and even more sophisticated synonym to go with each of the examples above, and use the new ones in the story.**

What Else Can We Do

✳ Students will take a generic photo of anything 'busy' at school. That is, a photo that has a lot going on in it. Show it on a white board.

✳ They may also find a 'busy' generic photo such as that of the New York City Skyline below. A photo such as this will lend itself to various possibilities when trying to find synonyms and antonyms.

✳ In groups of 4, students will find all the synonyms and antonyms that they can find in this photo and either put them on a list, or write them on the board. They may arrow them as well.

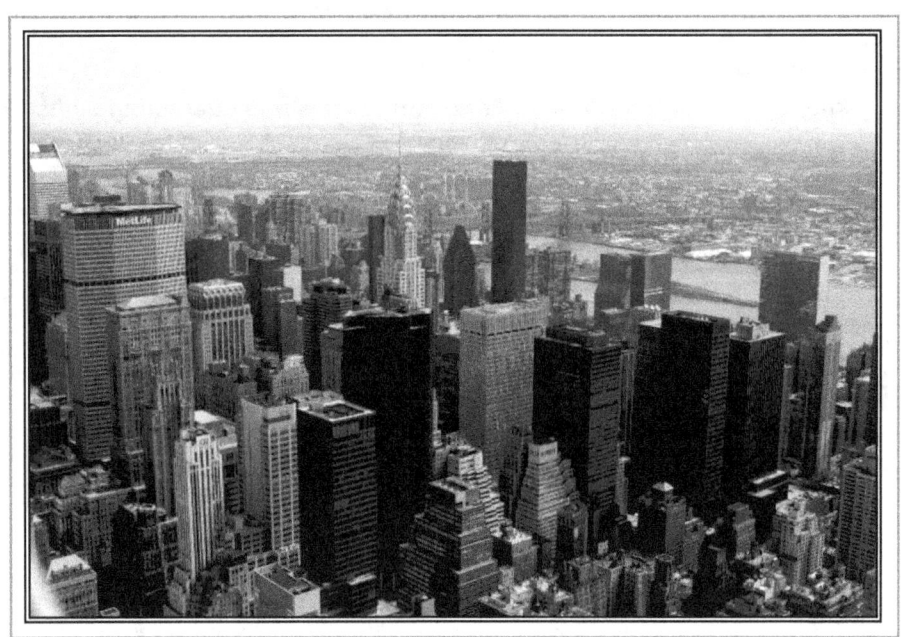

WHITE   POINTY

FAR   DRY

    IN   BLACK   FLAT

UP

      DOWN   OUT

WET

NEAR

38

Transitional Words and Phrases

Transitional words and phrases provide the glue that holds idea
together in writing.

Robert Harris

☞ *Students will practice using transitional words and phrases with candid
original photos.*

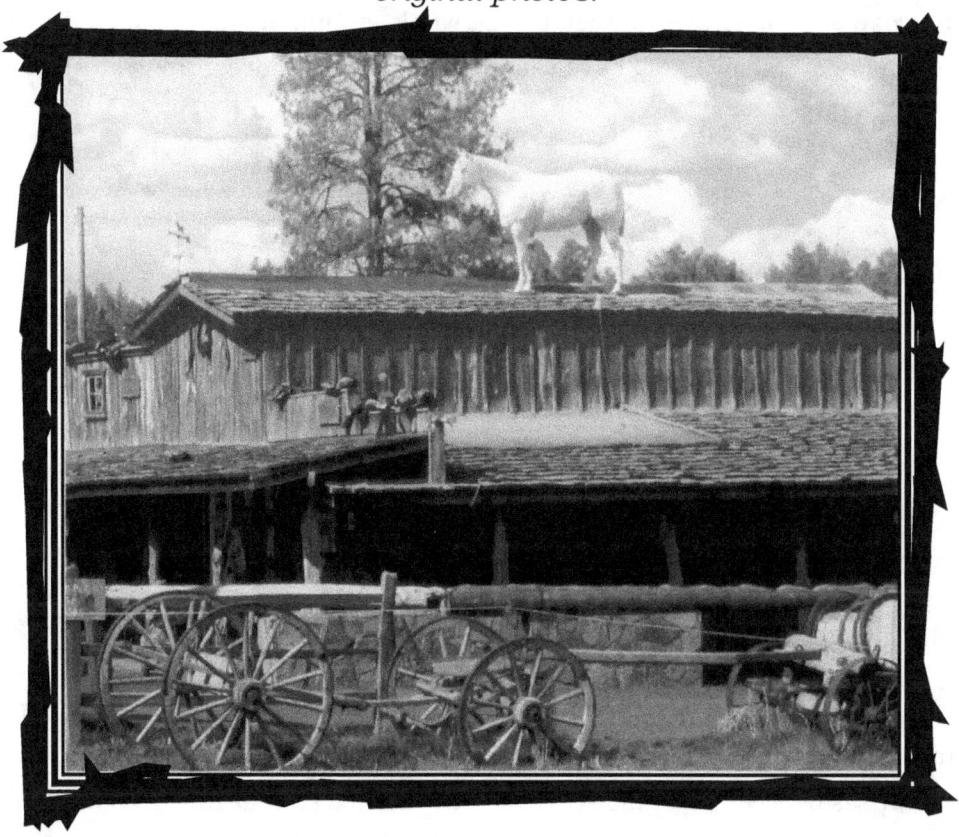

To Show Time - immediately, thereafter, soon, after a few hours, finally, then, later, previously, formerly, first (second, etc.), next, and then

To Repeat - in brief, as I have said, as I have noted, as has been note

To Emphasize - definitely, extremely, obviously, in fact, indeed, in any case, absolutely, positively, naturally, surprisingly, always, forever, perennially, eternally, never, emphatically, unquestionably, without a doubt, certainly, undeniably, without reservation

To Show Sequence - first, second, third, and so forth. A, B, C, and so forth. next, then, following this, at this time, now, at this point, after, afterward, subsequently, finally, consequently, previously, before this, simultaneously, concurrently, thus, therefore, hence, next, and then, soon

To Give an Example - for example, for instance, in this case, in another case, on this occasion, in this situation, take the case of, to demonstrate, to illustrate, as an illustration, to illustrate

To Summarize or Conclude – in brief, on the whole, summing up, to conclude, in conclusion, as I have shown, as I have said, hence, therefore, accordingly, thus, as a result, consequently

Here We Go

❏ Create a Languages Art moment by talking about, writing about, listening to others talk about and eventually reading about information and stories that come from the photo on the previous page.
❏ Select 3 parts of the photo that appeal to you and use *transitional words and phrases* that bond the three ideas together.
❏ Now ask a student to draw, cut out and paste onto the photo an object, a human or an animal
❏ The class will then use transitional words to legitimately include the added pasted object so that the addition makes sense in the 'whole' of things.

What Else Can We Do

✳ Have the students take a 'busy' photo such as the one on the following page. Create questions or directions that require students to *dissect* the photo and put *transitional words or phrases* between and among parts of the photos so that the ideas are connected. (See previous page).

1. ◯ = Use Compare and Contrast transitional words or phrases to meld ideas.

2. ⬡ = Use Cause and Effect transitional words or phrases to explain this section.

3. ↔ = Use transitional words that add ideas to this section.

4. ▢ = = Give transitional words or phrases that connect examples.

5. ▭ = Summarize the entire photo using correct summarization transitions.

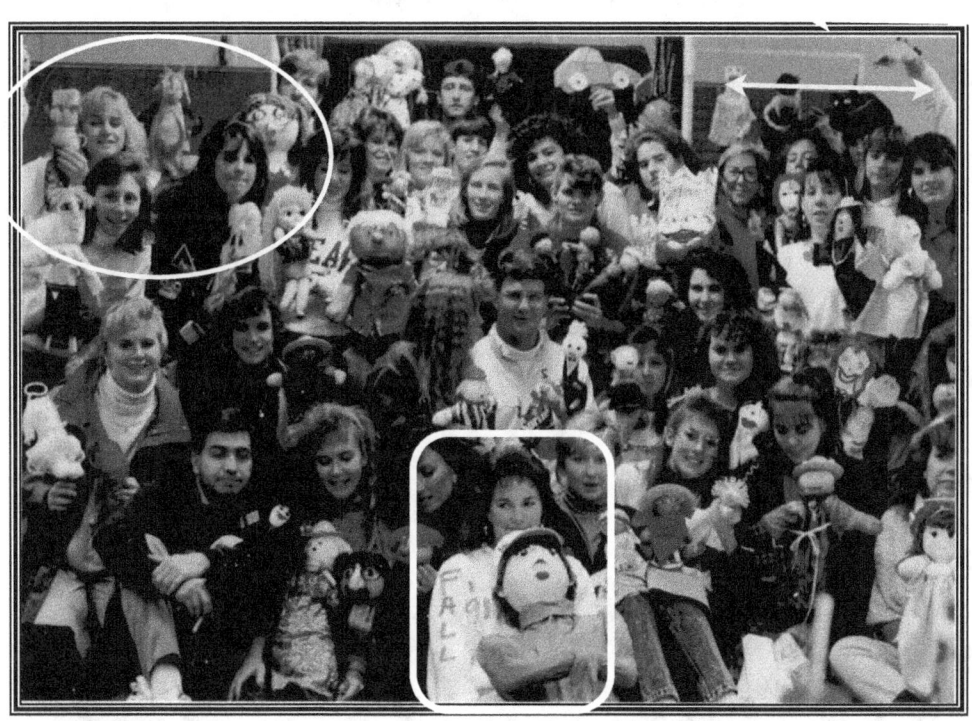

39
Two-Voice Poems

I read a dictionary once and thought it was a poem about everything.
Steven Wright

☛ Students will write two-voice poems with characters and
information found from certain photos.

SEA STARS

Sunbathing	
Sunbathing	
Resting on the coral rocks	
	And stones
Feeling the warm,	Warm rays beat down
Upon our wet and bumpy	
	Wet and veiny
Bumpy	Bumpy
Skin	Skin
The waves roll us in	In.. in.. tumbling in,
Toward the shore, and we	
	Cling
Cling, Cling	
The craggy, craggy	To the surface
Until the waves come again to the	Surface
And bring us to the cloak of water	Shore..to our rocks
	That becomes the
	safe harbor
Harbor	
Harbor	Harbor
	Harbor
Harbor of our	
Undersea	Undersea
Home	Home

90

Here We Go

❏ Read the previous two-voice poem and discuss the photo and what the two main 'voices' in the poem are trying to say.

❏ Take photos that show two main objects, animals, etc., which can be used for diverse points of view.

❏ Students, in pairs, will write a two-voice poem to accompany the photo.

❏ Students may want to shoot a photo with an animate and inanimate object and create a two-voice poem from that scenario as well.

What Else Can We Do

✳ Students will choose a photo or the one of the elephant on the following page. They will write a two voice poem using the elephant as the voice of the first poem and one of the following choices as the voice of the second poem.

Elephant Nose	Hunter	Tree	Jungle	Baby Elephant
Safari Guide	Lion	Zoo Keeper	Mate	River
Dentist	School Child	Camera	Vet	Noise

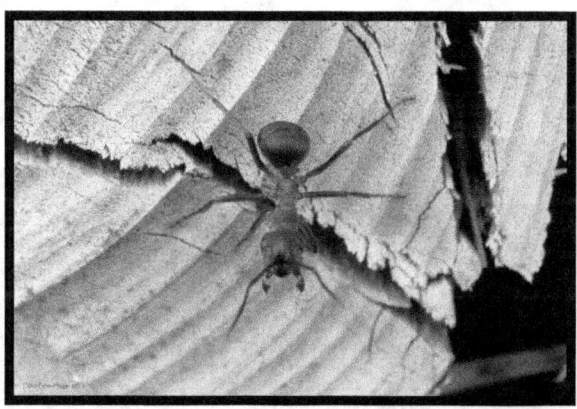

✳ Students will write two voice poems using characters that are opposite, as the ant above and the elephant on the following page. Focus on being different AND alike.

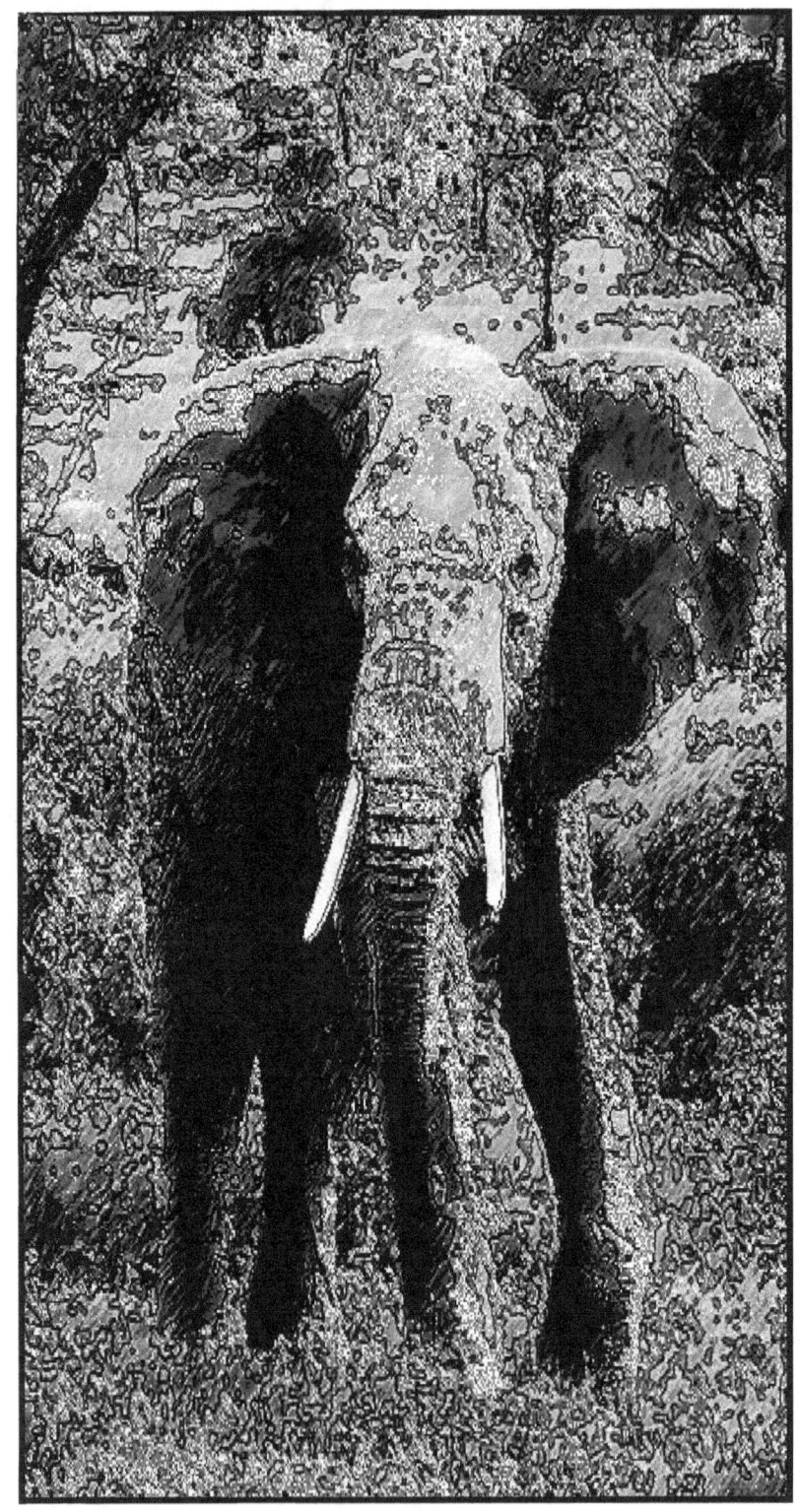

39
Voice

Voice...is what most people have in their speech but lack in their writing.
Peter Elbow

*Students will discuss various photos which relate in some way,
then write a brief story in their own words and voice.*

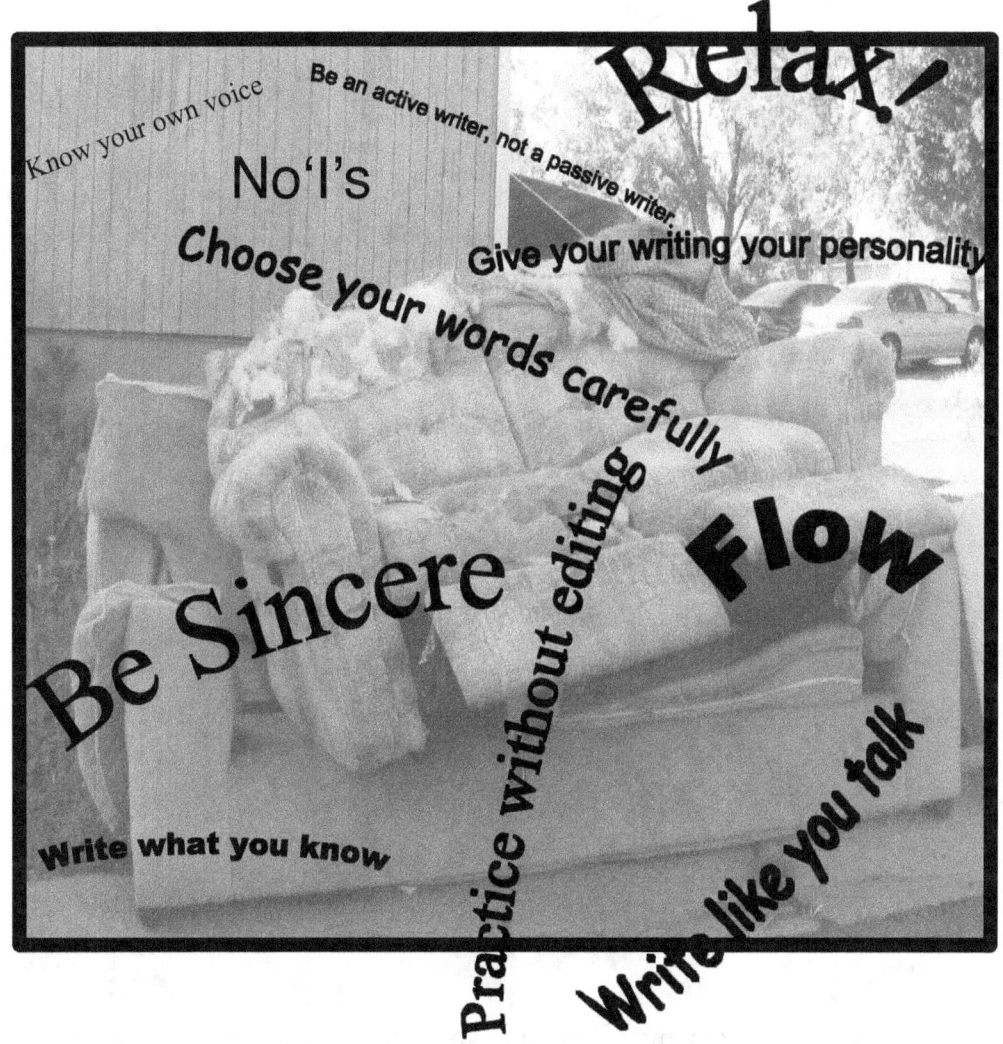

Know your own voice
Be an active writer, not a passive writer
Relax!
No 'I's
Give your writing your personality
Choose your words carefully
Be Sincere
Practice without editing
Flow
Write what you know
Write like you talk
Read out loud and hear how your writing sounds
Voice captures the sound of the individual

Here We Go

❏ You may not know an awful lot about old sofas as seen on the previous page, but if you look at that photo long enough, you will know something important about yourself, an experience, a dream, neglect, waste, poverty, pollution...something will come to mind that those beat up old couches trigger.

❏ Now find your own words, your own story, your own sincerity, and your own confidence and write that story as if it belongs to you, which it does. No I's, just the pure, interesting telling of a story between you and the reader.

❏ Finally, take a candid shot of something very, very important to you and write about it, in your own way, your own words, your own emotion.... your own voice.

What Else Can We Do

✱ Doors are intriguing. We always hope there is something interesting behind them - safe, mysterious, peaceful, chaotic, familiar, hidden, open to the universe, dangerous, melancholy, warm, familial, bizarre. There is always something there... beckoning us to step inside, with vision and words.

✱ Take a photo of a door, any door. Give students a chance to talk about factual and fictional experiences that those doors register.

✱ Using personal stories, students will tell a story about a certain door using the voice of 'who they were' when the door experience occurred.

✱ Then discuss the feeling of being 'outside the door compared to being 'inside' the door. Talk about chosen words used to express those feelings and those experiential moments. How did the words come to mind? What was difficult about staying true to the event? How did 'they' show themselves in the piece? What made this writing piece 'theirs'?

✱ Now, in pairs, take the photo and the writing and rethink the piece as if they 'both' entered the door. How do the two voices meld into one event?

INSIDE

OUTSIDE

FACT

FICTION

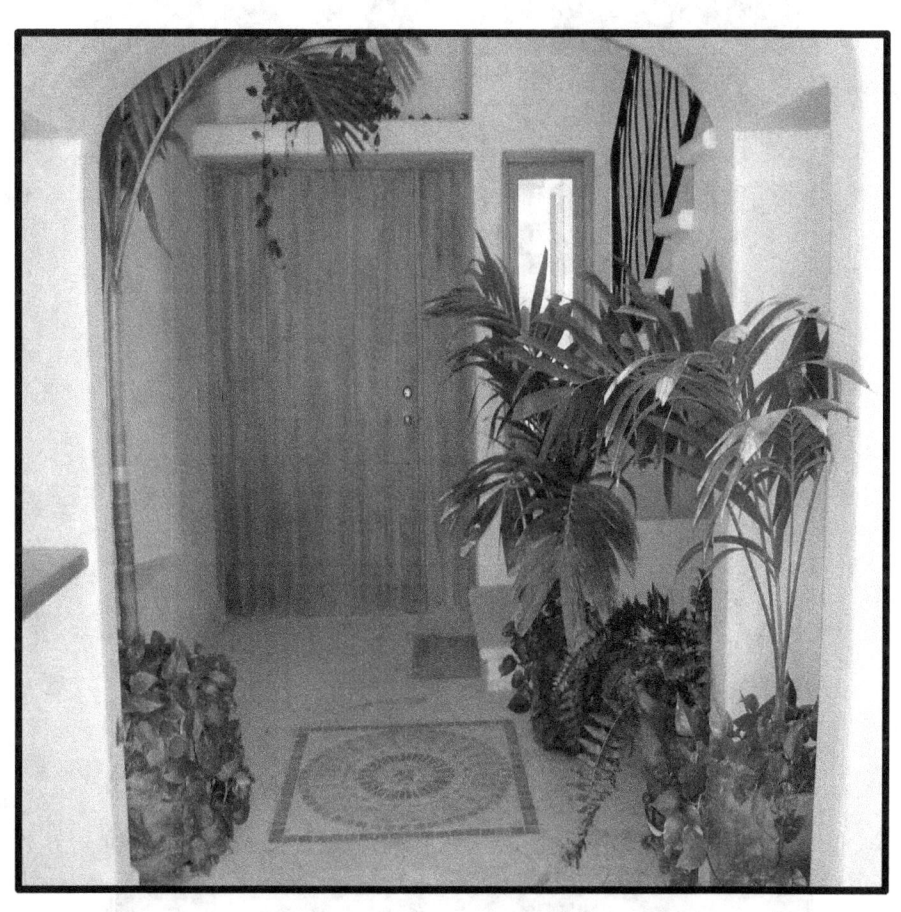

40

What Am I Missing
The details are not the details. They make the design.
Charles Eames

Students will practice finding details in photos and use the elements of photography to 'see' the details.

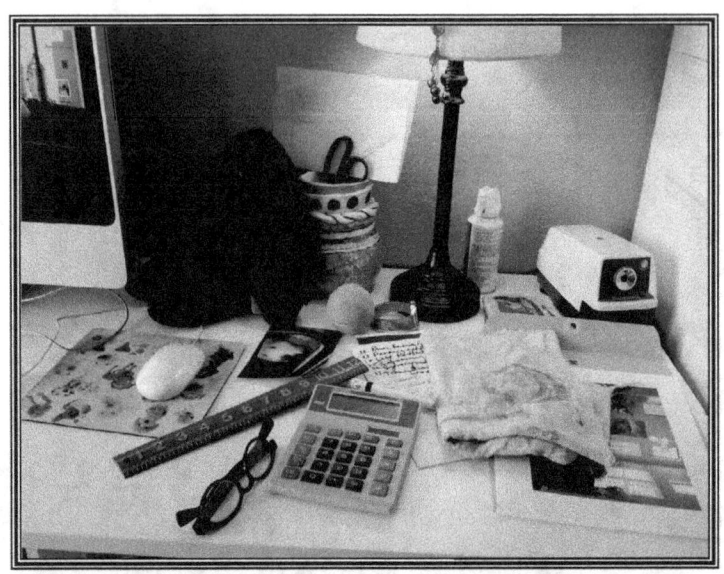

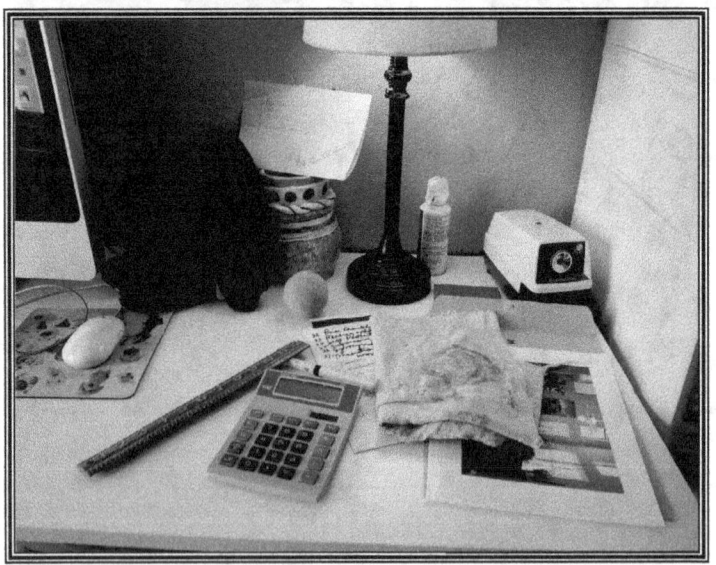

What is missing in the bottom photo?

Here We Do

❏ It's all in the details, or maybe not. Because if students look closely at the details of a certain photo they may begin to observe *the composition (how is it put together as a whole), harmony (*why do the separate facets of the photo work and flow, *balance (*why does it fit 'right' not 'out of kilter), order (*does the photo make sense in its structure) *and design (*does it work as a whole, are objects in the correct place) of that photo which really make it a 'living thing'.

❏ Look at the previous two photos and discuss those elements of photography explained above. Be specific.

❏ Select 10 objects from the class. Groups of 4 will take turns arranging them according to their understanding of the above elements. Put all of the photos out and critique as a class.

❏ Write on the board any descriptive or generally interesting words that come from the discussion

❏ Now just write as much as you can about one of the 'scenes'. Use the power of observation to create a

unique piece of writing that comes from observing and discussing the photos.

What Else Can We Do

✳ This book spends a lot of time on the importance of *observation* and the value of photography in bringing methods of observing into the classroom. Unfortunately, we as humans spend very little time observing, looking for details, seeing the whole picture, finding the hidden. Therefore, this last activity requires nothing but observation.

✳ Simply, one child per week, will bring in an original photo and put it on the bulletin board. Place a big sheet of chart paper near the photo. The children will simply observe everything they can in the photo; each object, shadow, cloud, item, design, geometric shape, mystery formation, and so on. Each of these 'observations' will be written on the chart paper. Now, ask the students what they wish to do with this information in terms of language arts. Give them time to do it.

ORGANIZING
Your
Photography Year

September SELF	October EMOTION	November HISTORICAL SCENES
December CULTURE	January BEGINNING MIDDLE and END	February WHAT'S WORTH WRITING ABOUT
March VOICE	April IMAGINATION	May MATH and PHOTOGRAPHY
June MY YEAR IN ONE PHOTO	?	?

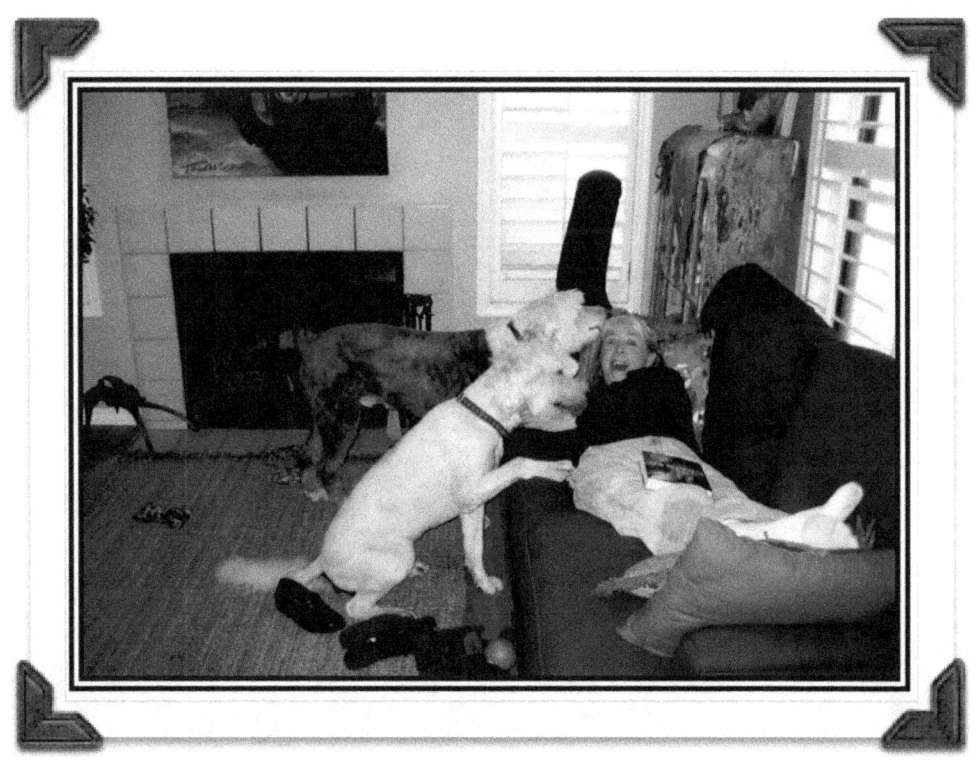

Martha Brady is Professor Emeritus at Northern Arizona University, in Flagstaff, Arizona. When she is not writing children's books or resource books for teachers, she is playing with her animals, reading on her Kindle, taking as many weekend trips as possible, and saving up for a canal trip through England. She had better hurry. She's old and won't use her hearing aids.

Martha's other books can be found on Amazon.Com

www.ingramcontent.com/pod-product-compliance
Lightning Source LLC
Chambersburg PA
CBHW080821180526
45168CB00006B/2528